Forms of Being

Forms of Being

Cinema, Aesthetics, Subjectivity

Leo Bersani and Ulysse Dutoit

 Publishing

This edition first published in 2004 by the
British Film Institute
21 Stephen Street
London W1T 1LN

The British Film Institute promotes greater understanding of, and access to, film
and moving image culture in the UK.

Cover design: ketchup
Cover illustrations: *The Thin Red Line* (© Twentieth Century Fox Film
Corporation), *Le Mepris* (courtesy StudioCanal Image) – see Picture Credits, p. 179.

Typeset in 11/16 point Adobe Caslon
by D R Bungay Associates, Burghfield, Berks
Printed by Cromwell Press, Trowbridge, Wiltshire

British Library Cataloguing-in-Publication Data
A catalogue record for this book is available from the British Library

ISBN 1 84457 015 0 (pbk)
ISBN 1 84457 016 9 (hbk)

Contents

Introduction: 'I don't see' (*Woe Is Me*)

A major virtue of the visual arts is their capacity to make the invisible visible. A virtue, and at times what appears to be an obsession, one analogous to the unsettling preoccupation with silence on the part of certain writers. Mallarmé formulated that preoccupation with his notion of *la page blanche*, but the page on which nothing is written is – in Mallarmé himself, as well as in writers otherwise as different from one another as Rilke, Crane, Celan and Beckett – a less impressive testimony to the importance of certain forms of verbal failure in literature than all those pages on which *silence is written*, pages on which (as Beckett puts it), unable to speak, the speaker can't help but continue speaking, but in words that somehow contain the inability to find words, even the desire not to find them. Analogously, Caravaggio's painting, as we have argued in *Caravaggio's Secrets*, frequently directs our look to spaces outside the painting itself, spaces designated as the necessary but unpainted extensions of certain formal elements within the work. A narrative representation – of a gypsy trying to read the lines in the palm of a young nobleman's hand in the Pinacoteca *Fortune Teller*, or of Christ in *The Calling of St Matthew* singling out the future saint from a group of seated men with a gesture summoning Matthew to follow him – is, if not dismissed, at least in danger of being subordinated to something more mysterious, less dramatic but perhaps also more compelling than the painting's 'story'. There is the implied extension, in *The Fortune Teller*, of a formal design initiated by certain correspondences between the two figures' garments (an extension into unrepresented spaces toward which the nobleman's gaze, bypassing the gypsy girl, directs our attention), and in the latter work, the highlighted gaze of the figure at the lower right toward some unpainted object of visual interest, a gaze and an object curiously dismissive of the work's portentous representational centre. It is as if Caravaggio were indeed intent on 'destroying painting', as Poussin complained, by means of an aesthetic of painting as under an obligation, at once ethical and ontological, to paint a call to invisibility at the heart of the visible world.[1]

That call is thematised in one of the works we will be discussing. The major point of contention between the two principal protagonists of Terrence Malick's *The Thin Red Line* is whether or not there is another world beyond this world. For Sergeant Welsh, the world we see is the only one there is, and it is a world of men killing one another, of a war about nothing more than 'property'. In defending Private First Class Witt's view that there is 'another world' (one he insists he has seen), Malick accepts the immense burden of somehow showing us a world that is not the one he films. Not only that: the film's 'argument' against the finality of war, of indefensible human violence, depends on the degree to which it succeeds in making that argument visually – more specifically, in making us see, in and through Witt's eyes, a world whose arguably unfilmable nature could easily be taken as proof of its non-being.

But let's suppose that *not being* has certain modes of visibility. This is the problematic wager of Jean-Luc Godard's 1993 film *Hélas pour moi* (*Woe Is Me*). The film begins with the arrival of a publisher named Abraham Klimt (Bernard Verley) in a Swiss community on Lake Geneva. He has come, as he says, in order to buy a story, but he doesn't know exactly what that story is. In order to get his facts right, he sets out to investigate what exactly happened on 23 July 1989. 'Exactly' is important, and absurd. (In a parody of Klimt's investigative ambitions, the phrase 'c'est exact' is said several times throughout the film.) For it turns out that the presumed facts of the story Klimt pursues are not only unfindable and perhaps inherently unknowable; more devastatingly, there may simply be no story to tell. Perhaps nothing at all happened. The case being investigated involves finding out if Rachel Donnadieu (Laurence Masliah) did indeed, as her name suggests, give herself to God on that July night, to God who would have borrowed the body of her husband, Simon (Gérard Depardieu), who left that day for an overnight business trip. Did Simon simply cut his trip short and come back home that evening, or did God, as one image suggests, slip into Simon's body and, thereby doubling Simon, profit from his absence in order to spend the night with his wife?

The film (in addition to its allusions to the Amphitryon myth) could be taken as a metaphysically clownish comment on detective stories were it not for the fact that the mystery under investigation is the anecdotal prop for an extraordinary visual and aural meditation on the relation between time and being. One of the film's most striking moments takes place while Simon and Rachel are seated next to each other before Simon leaves for his trip. What takes place is a spatial *dis*placement outside time. Simon suddenly disappears from the image; it is as if he were brutally yanked to the right and out of the frame, except that we don't see him *move* out of the frame. It is as if a cyclone sucked him away so rapidly that no transition can be traced between his presence and his absence. Godard's montage achieves a similar effect with Rachel a moment later, except that her non-transitional displacement occurs entirely within the framed scene. To the accompaniment of a jarring single chord of organ music, she is twice 'thrown' a few inches to the left of where she has been sitting. As in the case of Simon, she doesn't move from one position to another; rather, she simultaneously disappears and reoccurs to the side of herself. In both cases, it might seem that some positional 'mistake' were being corrected by an agent unconstrained by the distances between points. Being is transferred without being moved.

Since this scene comes shortly before the sequence of what may be Rachel's night with God, these bodily transfers could be thought of as an attempted visualisation of what a shift from one ontological register to another might be like. Godard makes visible the universe in which Rachel and God might mate not by showing us Simon the man in the act of leaving, but rather by juxtaposing Simon's presence with his disappearance; not by showing some transformation of Rachel, but rather by the very simple (and also somewhat brutal) trick of relocating her. Godard does not go so far as to suggest that relationality in the entire universe is affected by

Rachel's exact position on the bench (although such an argument could be imagined ...); he does, however, seem to be proposing a static yet sequential version (presence–absence, here–there) of ontologically doubled being – or, more exactly, of being at once empirical and metaphysical, or, also, of being at once realised (in the Rachel everyone knows) and potentialised (as the woman who may have mated with God). Neither position is final: Simon the man will return, and even in this scene Rachel is seen in her original position on the bench after her first transfer and before the second. The individual subject doesn't go *from* one register of being *to* another; what we are calling 'registers' could also be figured (although figuration fails us here ...) as parallel modes or lines of being, alternative unfoldings of events that don't 'communicate' with one another but inaccurately replicate one another. Simon 'lends himself' to his presence and to his disappearance (which will coincide with his reappearance as God), just as Rachel 'lends herself' to both positions on the bench. These immobile moves are at once ordinary and (as the musical chords suggest) catastrophic: the multiplication of the individual's positionality in the universe is, necessarily, a lessening or even a loss of individuality. We *are* not as distinct subjectivities but rather as that which gives *appearances* to different modes or functions of being. (In Godard's 1981 film *Passion*, this dispersal of subject-hood is proposed in social and political terms. The gestures of work, Isabelle [Isabelle Huppert] says, are the same as the gestures of love. She thus suggests that to transform the conditions of work, while necessary [she is leading a strike at the factory where she works], is less necessary than a reformulation of the being of work. The differences between love and work are operational; they have to do with instrumentalities [the manual repairing of a machine and the caressing of a body] rather than essences. The denial of the similitude reduces work to the purely mechanical and obscures the artfulness of love-making. The recognition of the similitude would orient specific reforms in the conditions of work toward a more generous acceptance of the erotics of work. It would, however, also mean that the working and the loving individual subjects would be individuated on the basis of their participation in a certain class of gestures which they would embody – gestures which, without them, would not appear.)

Like *Woe Is Me* and *Passion*, the films we will be considering propose the implausibility of individuality. The multiplication of being depends on a lessening of psychic subject-hood. More exactly, our reappearances *as* (mere) appearances depend on a certain type of withdrawal from realised being, a withdrawal we will associate with an aesthetic (rather than a psychological) subject. Near the end of *Woe Is Me*, we hear Klimt say: 'The rest took place beyond images and stories.' This is corrected by the travelling salesman who says he has just read Klimt's mind: 'Not beyond, but *this side of* the images and stories.' An equivalence is assumed here between images and stories. Let's propose something different: it is images that are 'this side of' stories. But what does 'this side of' – *en-deça de* – mean, *exactly*? The expression perhaps inevitably suggests temporality. We can imagine a non-temporal *au-delà*: something beyond, a transcendence that exists simultaneously with that which it transcends. *En-deçà*, on the other hand, can easily evoke a sequence: it suggests that which has not yet happened, a before-stories, for example, that will perhaps naturally realise itself as story. But this would be inconsistent with the way in which *Woe Is Me* treats the relation between past and present. Not only does the film fail to distinguish clearly between the two (certain events may have happened then, or may be happening now, during Klimt's visit: images are dispersed, 'thrown' at us in ways that make it impossible to say which ones belong to then, which ones to now; when were certain words said, before or after the words that precede them?).[2] More radically, temporal confusion is the sign of an identity between past and present. In Godard's ontology of time, there may be no before at all. 'The past', someone says in the film (the remark is taken up again in *Histoire(s) du cinéma*), 'is never dead. It's not even past.' How, then, might a non-past past be seen? One answer is that it can't be seen. Referring to the discovery of the Dutch physicist Jan Ort that visible matter constitutes only 50 per cent of the mass necessary for the force of the double pull of gravity in the universe, the narrator announces in voice-over that with this discovery 'phantom-matter was born, omnipresent but invisible'. The screen in *Woe Is Me* is frequently black; at one moment it is entirely occupied by the large capitalised words, 'JE NE VOIS PAS'. But perhaps the reason 'I don't see' anything is, as Simon insists to Klimt, because 'nothing happened [il n'est rien arrivé].' And yet we *have* seen all these un-happened events, although, as the visionary poetess Aude Amiel (Aude Amiot) says, 'seeing the invisible is exhausting'.

What is *en-deça* may, then, be an invisible non-event which, however, we can, with some effort, see. That effort is the work of spectatorship. It involves, first of all, allowing ourselves to be transferred from one mode of vision to another, to be jolted out of our ingrained habits of cinematic viewing. More than any other art form, film encourages us to believe in both the existence and the primordial importance of individuality. The film star is nearly always thought to be a sharply individualised presence; it remains a commonplace of film criticism to praise works that give us unforgettable individual characters, and to condemn those that fail to do so. And undoubtedly we owe part of our pleasure in going to the movies to the promise of a protected momentary intimacy (protected because all the presumed knowing of the other is on our side) with other persons massively and defencelessly exposed. So comforting is this expectation that in order to defeat it the film-maker must somehow traumatise our perception. Nothing explains Simon's disappearance from the frame or Rachel's displacement on the bench; they shock our visual habits, and in so doing at least begin to train us to look for Simon there where he is not, and to see Rachel elsewhere.

In the films we will be discussing, the subject's dispersal will come about, principally, through unexpected couplings – connections both to the human and to the non-human that are to the side of, or 'before' (*en-deça de*) more officially sanctioned connections that confirm such identities as husband, or mother, or soldier. Immanent in every subject is its similitudes with other subjects (and other objects) – similitudes that are illuminated, that 'shine' into visibility when those others intersect with the subject's spatial or temporal trajectories. Traumatised perception shatters the security of realised psychic and social identities; it makes visible traces of every body's limitless extensibility in both space and time. These connections are universally immanent. They make of the present no more of an event than the past is past, or has passed. Paul and Camille's marriage in *Contempt* is no more real than the marriage of Odysseus and Penelope – although they make the mistake of thinking of themselves as more real than their literary 'correspondents' and are therefore unable merely to *imagine* their identity as a passionately conjoined couple.

It would undoubtedly not have been, for them, a question of sustaining imaginary (as distinct from presumably real) being. We cannot become permanent works of art; the aesthetic subject is not a monumentalising of the self, but rather should be thought of as a renewable retreat from the seriousness of stable identities and settled being. As this suggests, the lightness of imaginary being is an ontological gain, but it is also a psychic loss. An artful ascesis is the precondition for a lessness that allows us to reoccur, differently, everywhere. But, as Pedro Almodóvar suggests, we really know very little about the viability of aesthetic subject-hood – about, most notably, the kinds of talk, of sociability, we have still to invent for relational regimes no longer dependent on identitarian myths. We have, after all, been richly nourished by those myths, and our at times exalted renunciation of them would be rather glib if it were not tinged by the melancholy of an always threatened silence and an always threatened blindness.

Notes

1. See Leo Bersani and Ulysse Dutoit, *Caravaggio's Secrets* (Cambridge, MA: MIT Press, 1998), Chapter 2.

2. Laetitia Fieschi-Vivet speaks perceptively of 'the disappearance of any chronologically based causality linking the shots' of the film in her essay, 'Investigation of a Mystery: Cinema and the Sacred in *Hélas pour moi*', in Michael Temple and James S. Williams (eds), *The Cinema Alone: Essays on the Work of Jean-Luc Godard 1985–2000* (Amsterdam: Amsterdam University Press, 2000), pp. 189–206.

15

1 Forming Couples (*Contempt*)

Contempt cements the couple. An arguably more plausible view would be that contempt drives the couple apart, a view supported – or so it has been maintained – by Jean-Luc Godard's 1963 film *Contempt*, in which a wife's sudden contempt for her husband deals the death-blow to an idyllic intimacy. The plausibility of this view depends on a rather simple yet irreproachable psychological reading: the feeling of contempt is incompatible with the sentiment of love. It is, in this respect, different from hatred of a loved object – hatred which, as our Western experts in passionate intimacy from Racine to Freud have shown, can generally be interpreted as the disguised expression of thwarted or guilty desire. Contempt, on the other hand, would be the blocking of *any* passionate attachment; indeed, it would depend on an act of judgment that at once presupposes and enacts the extinction of passion.

Godard himself perhaps invited such a reading when, in a 1963 interview, he spoke of the subject of his film as being 'people who look at one another and judge one another, and who are then in turn looked at and judged by cinema ...'[1] Looking is indeed central to *Contempt*, but the looks that express contempt as well as those that react to it, far from signifying the dissolution of the couple, reduce the entire

relational field to the structure of the intimately conjoined couple. This effect can be missed only if we identify with the apparently despised husband in Godard's film. Paul, the distressed object of contempt, obsessively seeks to understand why his wife now finds him contemptible, which for him means why she has turned away from him. He thus fails to see, in a sense we will presently elaborate upon, that she has never been closer to him. And criticism makes the same mistake when, rising above Paul's anguish but remaining nonetheless faithful to his perspective, it describes *Contempt* as 'a ceremony depicting a love lost', the breakdown of 'a complete and ideal love by instances of distrust'.[2] In other words, the interpretive point of departure for criticism, as for Paul, has been the destruction of the couple. The work of interpretation then consists of looking for the cause of the estrangement, a search conducted by Paul by means of his repeated, unsuccessful demand: 'Dis-moi pourquoi tu me méprises [Tell me why you feel contempt for me].'

We want to ask a very different question: what is the *appeal* of contempt, both for Camille and for Godard as a film-maker? This is by no means to suggest that Camille and Godard are, as it were, attracted to contempt for the same reasons. But in both cases we will be turning our attention away from the psychic origins of contempt and toward its effects in the world. In the case of Camille, this means examining the strategic advantages of contempt rather than the psychic events leading to a devastating ethical judgment. And in the case of the film-maker, the question can only be: what does contempt do to cinematic space? How does it affect the

21

visual field with which Godard works, and especially the range and kinds of movement allowed for in that space?

Paul Javal (Michel Piccoli), a writer whose unrealised ideal is to write for the theatre, is offered a well-paying job by the brash, vulgar, macho American producer Jeremiah (Jerry) Prokosch (Jack Palance). Prokosch is producing a film version of Homer's *Odyssey*; unhappy with the work of his director Fritz Lang (played by Fritz Lang), Prokosch wants to hire Paul 'to write some new scenes for the *Odyssey* ... not just sex ... but more ... more ...'[3] The producer, as Paul immediately sees, doesn't really know exactly what he wants 'more' of (except for the sex), but he probably means more of the sort of Hollywood spectacle with which Lang is of course only too familiar and which he apparently refuses to provide. Paul, whose sympathies will be with Lang rather than with Jerry, is nonetheless tempted to accept the latter's offer because, as Prokosch accurately and maliciously tells him, he needs the money and has a very beautiful wife. The wife is Camille, a twenty-eight-year-old former secretary (Brigitte Bardot), and Paul needs the money to pay for an apartment they have just bought in Rome (where the first two-thirds of the film takes place).

This potentially providential arrangement is endangered very early in the film when, invited by Jerry to come to his place for a drink after seeing some rushes from *The Odyssey* at Cinecittà, Paul encourages Camille to drive with Jerry in his red Alfa Romeo to the producer's home while he, Paul, will take a cab. This begins the fall from that happy period of their love when, as Camille says in a voice-over later on, 'Everything happened with a rapid, mad, enchanted spontaneity and I would

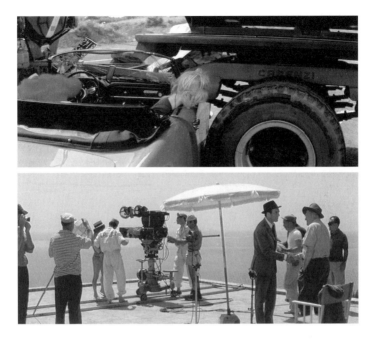

find myself once again in Paul's arms without remembering
what had happened.' Camille will now repeatedly look at Paul
with distrust and aversion, and, at the end of the extraordinary
scene in their apartment which takes up one third of the film
– a scene at once tedious, oppressive and brilliantly executed –
she announces to Paul that she no longer loves him, that in fact
she has only contempt for him. Camille nonetheless accompanies
Paul to Capri, where part of *The Odyssey* will be filmed. Her
contempt is perhaps irrevocably confirmed when Paul, repeating
his earlier, presumably despicable behaviour, encourages
Camille to return with Jerry to the producer's villa while he,
Paul, stays on the boat where Lang and his crew have been
shooting scenes from the Nausicaa episode in Homer. While
Camille will later say that she would rather die than reveal the

reasons for her contempt, and while Paul's unrelenting and anguished pressure can make her say nothing more specific than the accusation 'You're not a man', nearly all the film's spectators seem to share Paul's final speculation: Camille feels that Paul, sensing that Prokosch is attracted to her, has been encouraging her to be alone with the producer as a way of securing Jerry's professional good graces. Although Paul, hoping to convince Camille that her suspicions are unfounded, will announce his decision not to continue with the film (and to return to his writing for the theatre), Camille's contempt is unaffected by Paul's sacrifice and she accepts a ride back to Rome with Prokosch. The two are killed in a crash seconds after Jerry speeds his Alfa Romeo out of a service station onto the autostrada and into a truck. The film ends with Paul's farewell to Lang on the roof-terrace of the Villa Malaparte in Capri. Lang, who says that we must finish what we have begun, is shooting the scene of Odysseus' first view of Ithaca at the end of his ten-year voyage home from the Trojan War. Godard's and Lang's cameras approach one another by means of diagonal tracking movements from right to left; at the point where they are about to meet, Godard's camera continues its progress with a pan from right to left that leaves behind Lang and his crew (including Godard, who appears briefly as Lang's assistant) and the actor playing Odysseus who is filmed from behind, arms raised, looking over the sea toward his homeland. The final image, in which we do *not* see Ithaca, is a still of the sea and the sky; we hear the word 'Silence!' twice (once in French, and once in Italian), and the word 'FIN', in blue letters against a black background, will itself disappear in a final black dissolve.

We risk the tedium of this plot summary in order to emphasise the unpromising and improbable nature of the film's 'story'. While the vast number of interviews Godard has given – and especially the more recent ones – bring an invaluable perspective to his work as a film-maker, some of his comments about *Contempt* don't take us much further than the presumed psychological or ethical lesson to be learned from this story. The film, he claimed in an interview from the same year the work came out, should give us 'a fleeting feeling of the vanity of all things'. *Contempt* is about men cut off from the gods and from the world, and the drama of Camille and Paul is that of a chance misunderstanding that somehow ends in catastrophe.[4] Such statements might describe the mediocre novel by Alberto Moravia, *Il disprezzo*, from which the film was taken, but it has nothing to say about the confrontation between that novel, which also includes the account of a filmic version of *The Odyssey*, and the Godard film which at once imitates and betrays the relation in the novel between the doomed contemporary couple and the filming of the ancient epic that celebrates the marriage of Odysseus and Penelope. Godard was aware of the poor quality of his literary source. He called Moravia's novel a common *roman de gare* – the kind of book you buy before boarding a train – 'full of classical and outmoded feelings, in spite of the modernity of the situations. But,' he added, 'it's with that kind of novel that beautiful films are often made.'[5]

What is the secret of this cinematic alchemy? Godard puts into question the interest and even the ethical validity of a subject treated by Moravia with great seriousness: desire and lost love. Moravia's work unintentionally parodies the literature of desire and of psychological analysis to which it belongs. While exploiting a mildly clever analogy and contrast between the desire-ridden modern couple and the (presumably) psychologically neutral couple of Homer's world, Moravia manages to make of that contrast nothing more than the melancholy and mystified longing of a psychologically saturated consciousness. Godard is also interested in the relation to Homer – especially, it would seem, in the connections between the modern couple's estrangement and Odysseus and Penelope's marriage. His film implicitly asks how the modern couple 'remembers' the ancient couple, and in so doing it proposes an original and valuable view of any presumed relation to the past. Both the film and the novel offer an interpretation of Odysseus and Penelope's marriage in which it prefigures the troubled union of Camille and Paul in Godard, and Riccardo and Emilia in Moravia. This reading is proposed by the German director Reingold in *Il disprezzo*; it is initiated by Prokosch and stubbornly and unconvincedly elaborated by Paul in *Contempt*. The intellectually smug Reingold insists on modernising *The Odyssey*, by which he means dissecting it, examining its internal mechanism, and putting it together again, as he says, 'according to our modern requirements'. These requirements are, unsurprisingly, psychological or, more specifically, psychoanalytic: 'we shall', Reingold promises, or warns, Riccardo, 'explore the mind of Ulysses – or rather, his subconscious'.[6] The dissection and exploration lead to an interpretation echoed by Paul in his

conversation with Lang in Capri. Reingold summarises his
findings for Riccardo:

psychoanalytic interp of Odyssey

> Point one: Penelope despises Ulysses for not having reacted like
> a man, like a husband, and like a king, to the indiscreet behav-
> iour of the Suitors ... Point two: her contempt causes the
> departure of Ulysses to the Trojan War ... Point three: Ulysses,
> knowing that he is awaited at home by a woman who despises
> him, delays his return as long as he can ... Point four: in order to
> regain Penelope's esteem and love, Ulysses slays the Suitors ...
> d'you understand, Molteni?[7]

Godard gives to Lang Riccardo's refutation of this psychologising rewriting of *The Odyssey*, a refutation that implicitly
appeals to the theory of epic objectivity developed by Hegel
in the section of the *Aesthetics* devoted to poetry. Lang's
argument repeats almost word for word this impassioned
response on the part of Riccardo to Reingold's reading of
Homer:

> The beauty of the *Odyssey* consists precisely in the belief in reality
> as it is and as it presents itself objectively ... in this same form,
> in fact, which allows of no analysis or dissection and which is
> exactly what it is: take it or leave it ... In other words ... the
> world of Homer is a real world ... Homer belonged to a civilis-
> ation which had developed in accordance with, not in antagonism
> to, nature ... That is why Homer believed in the reality of the
> perceptible world and saw it in a direct way, as he represented it,
> and that is why we too should accept it as it is, believing in it as

object reality

dns (role of hidden mngs. [handwritten note in margin]

Homer believed in it, literally, without going out of our way to look for hidden meanings.[8]

Godard obviously sympathises with Lang, but, as we shall see, his film is also ironic about any secure view of the past; it implicitly puts into question the assumption that the past is finished and that it can therefore be known. In *Il disprezzo*, on the other hand (which is narrated in the first person from Riccardo's point of view), nothing indicates that Moravia takes any distance either from Riccardo's view of Homer in the passage just quoted or from the extremely muddled and self-serving application of that view, at the end of the novel, to Emilia and himself. Godard, happily, simply ignores that application; it has something to do with Riccardo now belonging to an 'ideal

world', to which, through his reading of Homer as belonging to the 'real world', he somehow aspires. He is determined to raise Emilia to his level, Emilia who is seen at once as having the simplicity and genuineness of nature and the miserable conventionality of 'the perfectly real world of people like Battista and Reingold'.[9] Most tellingly, Moravia's sympathy with the non-psychological relationality of Homer's world has no effect on the kind of novel he writes. Riccardo's sense of impotence – his sentimentalising distancing of the Homeric as something ideal and inaccessible, something that doesn't exist but to which he should nonetheless aspire – is echoed in Moravia's own inability to take any distance at all from his psychological fiction. Godard, instead of simply lamenting our imprisonment in a psychologised consciousness, will make us see both the damage done to the relational field by that consciousness *and* the possibility of a field in which relational lines might be drawn differently.

Il disprezzo oppressively repeats, from beginning to end, Riccardo's anguished curiosity about the reasons for Emilia's contempt. It is, in other words, a novel about the impenetrability of the other's desires – just, we might say, as much of Proust's great novel is. But Moravia never asks the more interesting questions to which this curiosity might give rise, such as: what is the relation between passion itself and the loved one's turning away from the lover? Can the pursuit of the other's desires avoid becoming a crisis of *self*-identification? In what sense might the estrangement of the passionate couple be said to reveal the estrangement constitutive of passionate coupling itself (thus confirming Lacan's famous dictum: 'There is no sexual relation')? We are not saying that Moravia should have asked exactly these (Proustian) questions, but we are saying that if his novel is a *roman de gare*, it is because it is never more than the story it tells, because he is never pressured by that story into a speculation on the nature of its elements – about, specifically in this case, the nature of sexual passion. Its thematic subject is all there is. *Il disprezzo* is the hothouse preservation of the psychological novel after that novel had been dissolved, as an explorable genre, by the climactic dissections of Proust.

Any such dissection would have depended on the impenetrable Emilia being put into sharper focus. The question of *what contempt does* can only be answered if the contemptuous subject's remoteness and passivity are demystified. This is not at all the same as asking why Emilia or Camille feel contempt. Moravia does show us that Emilia's contempt immobilises Riccardo in his passion, but nothing much can be made of that demonstration unless it expands into a critique of contempt itself. Godard has said that he had originally wanted Kim Novak for the role of Camille. Novak has, he added, 'a passive, placid character … a soft character. Her mystery is her softness.' That's a good description of Moravia's Emilia, but it's a bad description of Godard's Camille – that is, of Brigitte Bardot. In the same interview, Godard recognises this when he specifies that '[Camille's] character came from what is Bardot.' Unlike Paul, 'whose psychology can be justified – on a purely psychological level', Bardot is 'a block. You have to take it as a block, all in one piece. That's why it's interesting.'[10] Bardot couldn't be transformed into Camille; Godard had to take her as Bardot, to let her simply be.

And how was she? There is an amusing reference to Bardot within the film when, in response to Camille's asking for the source of one of his literary quotations, Lang identifies it as 'an excerpt from a ballad by poor B.B.' Paul asks, 'Bertold Brecht?' just as Camille, with the trace of a smile, walks out of the frame and Lang answers, 'Yes.' Camille is Bardot-ised more spectacularly, and more significantly, in the film's opening scene, the one wholly contempt-free sequence. At the insistence of Joe Levine, the film's executive producer, who apparently thought there wasn't enough of Bardot in the film – of what Bardot, at the height of her fame, was most famous for – Godard added this scene of the naked Bardot lying in bed next to Paul. The

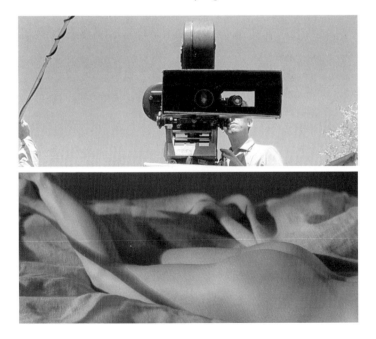

sequence immediately follows the film's credits, which are given not as a written text (except for the title, *Le Mépris*, red letters on a black background), but in voice-over. The recital of the credits is visually accompanied by a scene that, at the very beginning of the film and in a very literal way, brings the mechanics of film-making, and of film-looking, to the forefront of our attention. A Mitchell camera is shown moving toward us on tracks from the right background. The cameraman and two technicians are filming Francesca, Prokosch's assistant (Georgia Moll), as she walks toward us to the left of the tracks. When the camera arrives just in front of where it is being filmed by Godard's camera, it makes a 45-degree pan to the left so that it is facing us and then tilts downward until it and Godard's camera, which has been filming the scene from below, are directly framing each other. Godard's camera films Coutard's camera filming it. At the very beginning of *Contempt* – even 'before' *Contempt* – this sequence threatens the visual impunity we generally enjoy in looking at films. In the darkness of the movie-house, we alone do the looking; the filmic images can't look back at the spectator's protected, intact body. The title sequence of *Contempt*, by emphasising the physicality of the filming process, paradoxically brings that process close to theatre, where the spectator, although also 'lost' and inviolate in a darkened room, must always confront real bodies who at any moment may really move toward him, as Coutard's camera moves toward us. While Coutard is of course not filming the spectator's body, his camera has captured our point of view; it is looking at the site/sight of our looking, which it has reduced to the unidentifiable circle of light we see in Coutard's lenses.

And at this very moment the narrative voice perversely gives us this perhaps apocryphal quote from André Bazin as a gloss on the meaning of the film we are about to see: 'Cinema … substitutes for our look a world in accord with our desires. *Contempt* is the story [or history: *l'histoire*] of that world.' We say 'perversely' because the passage is recited just at the moment when we can no longer delude ourselves into thinking that film – inherently a double operation of projection and reflection – will not only allow us to look at, to visually appropriate the world without being looked at ourselves, but that it will also accommodate the desires that inform our looking. The exhilarating prospect that knowledge of the real – already a fantastic gain – will become the recognition of a world modelled on our desires is erased by the look directed at us by a camera-subject ignorant of and indifferent to our desires.

It is, however, immediately after the (pseudo-)Bazin quote that we see the specular ideal it expresses momentarily realised. Camille, lying naked face down on their bed, asks Paul if he loves her body, more exactly all the parts of her body, beginning with her feet and ending with her facial features. Interestingly, however, she doesn't tell him to look directly at her body. Instead, she begins by asking him if he can see her feet and her behind in the mirror – so that what Paul responds to (except for her face) is either his memory of those parts of Camille's body not reflected in the mirror or a framed reflection of her body. The austere warning of the title sequence is undermined by Camille's removal of herself from the real space of the bed she and Paul are lying on, of the room they are in, indeed of all the unmappable space they, like all human subjects, inhabit. By

[handwritten margin notes: "unsettling the spectator." and "give Bardot as an icon."]

35

placing herself, at the very start of the sequence, within the framed security of the mirror, she defines the conditions of Paul's, and our, looking at her. Godard has given Levine Bardot with a vengeance – not simply the erotically luscious Bardot, but the visual icon that drew millions of desiring gazes to her body. The iconic power is meticulously reaffirmed through all those questions (which become fairly detailed: 'What do you prefer,' Camille asks, 'my breasts or the tips of my breasts?' – to which the compliant but perhaps slightly befuddled Paul responds: 'I don't know – both [c'est pareil]'). This interrogation, far from putting Bardot's body into non-totalisable pieces, seems meant to guarantee that nothing will escape being desired, that Paul's final summary of his love will be, as indeed it is, all-inclusive: '*Camille*: So you love me totally! *Paul*: Yes. I love you totally, tenderly, tragically.' This is followed by the somewhat ambiguous concluding remark from Camille: 'Moi aussi Paul.'

The CinemaScope of *Contempt* could easily have been complicit with this splendid narcissistic display: it might have given fabulous space to the fabulous body. However, even if this were the case, Lang's dismissive reference later on to CinemaScope as 'not made for men, it's made for serpents, for burials' would have retroactively inserted a sinister association – with Eve and the satanic serpent of the Garden of Eden – into the scene celebrating the naked Camille's desirability. But Godard's camera doesn't in fact celebrate that desirability with the generous visual dimensions of the cinemascopic screen. If Camille is verbally aiming at totality, the camera is more reticent: her whole body never occupies the screen, whose immense space is partly filled by ... the head of the bed on which they are lying! The camera pans over the parts of her body, some of which are even obscured by shadows. Godard also manages partially to redirect our attention from Bardot's body to his own formal devices: the red and blue filters that impose uniformity on the colours, the slow tracking shots along Bardot's body.[11]

The imprisoning psychic and physical space into which Camille's contempt draws Paul is prefigured by the mirror in which his enraptured gaze visually seals a total, tender and tragic love. In that mirror, Camille becomes for Paul the eminently filmable image she is for us, an image no longer subject to the existential constraints – the visual discontinuities, displacements and distractions – of real space. Contempt is the psychic version of this erotic strategy. In *Caravaggio's Secrets*, we used Jean Laplanche's category of the enigmatic signifier to designate a mode of address (evoked by Caravaggio's early portraits of boys with erotically provocative poses and looks) in which the relational and visual fields are reduced to a couple immobilised by seduction, fascination and paranoia. The enigmatic signifier is Laplanche's term for an adult world infiltrated with unconscious and sexual significa-tions and messages by which the child is seduced but which the child can't understand. The inability to decipher the other as enigmatic signifier constitutes us as sexual beings – that is, beings in whom desire or lack is central. Desire as lack is born, we argue, as the exciting pain of a certain ignorance: the failure to penetrate the sense of the other's soliciting – through touch, voice, gesture or look – of our body. The enigmatic signifier

narrows and centres our look; it is the originating model of a relationality in which subject and object are separated by the distance of an imaginary secret or a special authority, a distance that only 'knowledge' might cross or eliminate.

This is the distance created by Odette in a single night in Proust's *Swann's Way*. Failing to appear at a party where Swann had expected her, and not to be found in the cafés and on the boulevards of a city Proust compares to 'the realm of darkness', where, 'as though among the phantoms of the dead', the panicky Swann might have been 'searching for a lost Eurydice', Odette is transformed from an object of sensual interest into an object of erotic fascination.[12] In Godard's film, contempt is the means by which Camille, now an enigmatic signifier, 'promotes' Paul's desire for her to the status of a total, inescapable and permanent passion. The initiating move of this strategy takes place in a scene that is most frequently discussed in terms of *Paul's* behaviour. We refer to the moment when, in the face of Camille's apparent astonishment and irritation, Paul encourages her to get into Prokosch's car and to drive alone with him to the producer's home. This, presumably, is the moment of 'misunderstanding' – a misunderstanding that will somehow blossom into estrangement and catastrophe. To look at the sequence of events in this manner is to make of Camille a figure much less interesting than she actually is. It reduces her to the stupid conventionalism that does seem to characterise Moravia's Emilia: this single, at least possibly innocuous gesture on Paul's part would be enough to make her conclude that he is not a 'man' and to give birth to her implacable and irreversible sentiment of contempt. To give some plausibility to the gap between cause and effect here, we would have to engage in the aesthetically irrelevant exercise of speculating on the hidden tensions in their love before this moment – tensions that nothing in the film authorises us to suppose. Camille – as well as the major visual and structural tensions of the film – becomes much more interesting when we note that she is far from being a passive agent in this scene. Camille does not exactly disguise her activity, but the success with which she makes everyone – in and out of the film – fail to notice it can partly be measured by the description of this scene in the scenario of *Contempt* published by the French review *L'Avant-scène*. In front of the Cinecittà studio where rushes from *The Odyssey* have just been shown, Paul introduces Camille to Jerry, who, sitting in his car, shakes her hand, looking

away from her. Camille is then introduced to Lang, and she, Paul and Lang speak for a moment to the right of Jerry's car, whose motor can be heard during their exchange. While Paul goes on speaking to Lang, Camille turns away from them and goes back to Jerry's car. *L'Avant-scène* tells us that she then moves along the car and goes around it – failing to mention that, looking down at the car as she does so, her fingers glide along its surfaces so that, when she reaches the other side, she will have caressed nearly all of this metallic extension of Prokosch's body. The continuously revved-up red Alfa Romeo is presented so obviously, even so crudely, as a manifestation, a tool of Jerry's machismo – a tool that, in its final thrust forward at the end of the film, will kill both Jerry and Camille – that it hardly seems exaggerated to speak of Camille initiating a carnal contact between the two of them in the early scene.[13] Her speech of course suggests just the opposite – the opposite in fact of any activity at all. Her preferred responses to questions – will she come for a drink to Jerry's house? will she accompany Paul to Capri? – are: 'I don't know', 'Perhaps' and 'My husband will decide.'

The scene just discussed interests us less as a sign of an erotic attraction to Jerry than as a ritual-like enactment of Camille's power to imprison a fascinated gaze, a power that contempt consolidates. Contempt immobilises Paul's gaze, afflicting it with a paranoid intensity: what has he done to make himself contemptible in Camille's eyes? Paul has been stolen from himself; he is now a secret in Camille's eyes. The brilliant success of contempt as an affective strategy depends on an apparent contradiction: it fixes its object's gaze on itself at the same time that it remains invisible. By manoeuvring Paul into looking at her in order to find his own contemptible image, Camille enjoys the double advantage of being the nearly exclusive object of his look and *of not being seen.* Contempt blinds the other at the very moment it intensifies his visual attention. Contempt could thus be considered, more generally, as the psychic metaphor for a body so secure in its power to dazzle the gaze of others that it can count on not being observed. It is as if Camille–Bardot knew that our transfixed look would not *see* the way she circles Prokosch's car ...

The extraordinarily narrowing effect this has on the fields of vision of both the subject and object of contempt is brilliantly rendered in a scene on the roof terrace of Jerry's villa (the Villa Malaparte) in Capri. The first shot shows us Camille sitting on the terrace, with the sea and the sky beyond and above her. She gets up and moves left a few steps toward the centre of the terrace, stops and waves with both arms toward the right in the direction of the cliff along whose paths Paul and Lang have been walking, discussing *The Odyssey.* She takes a few steps to the right again, and, as the music that has been accompanying her movements stops, she hastens her step and walks out of the frame at the end of a 90-degree pan to the left. The camera stops for a few seconds in a long shot of the sea, the sky and, in the left half of the frame, the cliff. We then hear Paul calling 'Camille!' just before he enters from where she has just exited. He at first retraces Camille's steps on the terrace followed by the same camera movement, but in reverse, that had traced Camille's exit. (How could they have missed each other ...?) In their self-absorption, in their search

for and flight from one another, they execute the only movements in the sequence, movements curiously detached from
the natural setting against which they take place. In a vast
context of great stillness, their preoccupied crossing of the
terrace (with Paul repeating Camille's itinerary in the opposite
direction) has something mechanical and incongruous. They
move without seeing anything around them, and this disconnectedness has the effect of making the cliff, the sea and the
sky seem almost like a painted backdrop. It is not exactly that
nature becomes insignificant; indeed, when it is framed as a
mere view into which these unseeing, inattentive human
figures are deposited, the natural scene becomes just that, a
mere scene which, however, perhaps by virtue of this violation
of its presence, takes on a somewhat ominous, threatening

aspect. (A similar effect is given by the splendid but deadening framed views of the sea and the cliff through the windows of the Villa Malaparte, a structure somewhat prison-like in its magnificent promontory setting.) What Lang alludes to as the neurosis of modern man (and of the modern couple), and which Jerry and Paul project onto Odysseus and Penelope, is not simply a social or psychic phenomenon. Godard positions it within the spaces of nature, suggesting that it profoundly modifies our relation to those spaces by blocking them with dissonant human presences. A blocking that is also a kind of emptying: neurotic desire – which may be a tautology – creates voids in space. The lack inherent in the desire that at once separates and cements the passionate couple is replicated by spatial breaks at those points where, as it were, their bodies tear into space. Space becomes discontinuous when it is invaded by these foreign bodies whose inner habitat has the false extensibility of a purely psychic space.

The roof-terrace of the Villa Malaparte resembles an enormous stage. And Godard films Camille's and Paul's entrances and exits as if his camera were constrained by theatrical vision, as if, like the spectators in a theatre, he couldn't follow them into the 'wings' into which Camille disappears and from which Paul emerges. This is only one of several references to theatre in *Contempt*, and we might explain Godard's easy moves between the theatrical and the cinematic by referring to his claim, in a 1968 interview, that there is 'no difference between the theater and movies. It is all theater.' But, as he goes on to say, 'it is simply a matter of understanding what theater means'.[14] And theatre means differently in film and on the stage. 'It is all theater' may be nothing more than a way of reminding us that while theatre can do without film, film can't do without theatre. In film, only the most thoroughly discontinuous and unrealistic (or surrealist) succession of images might succeed in being wholly inhospitable to presentation on a stage. There are, however, major differences. Not only is our relation to bodies as images necessarily different from our relation to real bodies present at the time we are seeing them; the filmic medium may also be intrinsically uncongenial to certain major forms of theatrical drama. While films, for example, can of course imitate theatrical time and thereby submit to the temporal irreversibility necessary for tragedy, film also makes possible a very different, non-tragic time. The time of tragic drama is inexorably narrativised time; temporal sequence in film, on the other hand, is the result of a decision. It is, more precisely, an effect of montage, which may make it difficult for someone like Godard, who has spoken of montage as the defining feature of film as an art form, to take seriously the *necessity* inherent in tragedy. *Contempt*, which Godard characterised as 'un peu hollywoodien', is his most classical, realistic film, and it thereby seems to obey the narrative rule of temporal irreversibility. But, interestingly, Camille's and Jerry's deaths are not the film's climax; it ends, instead, with the shooting of a scene from Lang's film followed by a shot that (we will return to this) is outside both the narrative of *Contempt* and the narrative of *The Odyssey*. And yet something we might call the tragic is central to *Contempt*, although it should not be defined in either affective or ethical terms. It rather has something to do with the human disconnecting

but does not obey entirely.

itself from the space it inhabits. The loss or the violation of space is the loss of the filmic itself. The tragedy of the modern couple's claustrophobic self-absorption is its destructive effect on what surrounds them – or, more exactly, on the film-maker's ability to compose a relatedness between the human and the non-human. Camille and Paul sin against the cine-mascopic; to film *them*, perhaps only the close-up would be entirely appropriate.

And yet the close-up is an ambiguous means of characteris-ation, or even of identification. In *Arts of Impoverishment*, we discuss the last sequence of Alain Resnais's *Mon oncle d'Amérique* as a powerful illustration of the *dis-* or *mis-*identifying effects of visual *rapprochement*. The film ends with eight still shots of a brick wall, a wall on which a forest has been painted. Each shot, in abrupt and discontinuous transition from one fixed angle of vision to the next, brings us closer to the wall while thrusting upon us the ambiguity of the object being approached. The closer we get to the wall, the less we see. Not only is the narrowing of the field of vision made disorienting by the spaces on the wall that are skipped from one still to the next; it also becomes more and more difficult to describe the wall itself. We are shifted from a subject (a building with a scene from nature painted on it) to elements of construction. We recognise a building, but then the camera focuses on a giant tree, then on tree trunks, and finally to spots of paint on the bricks. We become more and more conscious of the bricks through the forest, and the trees finally disappear into the building, the human edifice, which is their only reality. And yet the final shot of a single brick brings us back to the earth from which the entire building has been made. The wall's identity is unlocatably somewhere between nature and artifice: it is nature composed, constructed, a nature we see representing itself *as* nature.[15]

Even more radical effects can be obtained when the camera approaches a human face. Speaking of the mysterious resemblance between the two women's faces in Bergman's *Persona*, Gilles Deleuze writes that the close-up has pushed the face 'into those regions where the principle of individuation no longer holds sway'. Bergman simultaneously films the face and its erasure, 'the fear of the face confronting its own nothingness'. *Contempt* stops short of filming what Deleuze calls 'the nihilism of the face',[16] but the close-ups of Camille and Paul are either psychologically inexpressive or psychologically impenetrable. If we read 'contempt' into the close-ups of Camille's face, it is because the film's title and Camille herself (when she reveals her contempt to Paul) have identified the film's apparent subject for us. In fact, there are shots of her – perhaps especially when she looks fixedly and silently at Paul in the garden of Jerry's home in Rome – in which she resembles the statues of the gods from Lang's *Odyssey*: still, immobile and impenetrable. To say that these looks express contempt, or a mixture of aversion, astonishment and distress (as well as a silent and desperate appeal to Paul), is to speculate, as Paul is forced to do, on what the enigmatic signifier is concealing. Even with Paul, the close-up can be psychologically mystifying. Having settled into a chair on the boat from which scenes for *The Odyssey* are being filmed, and encouraged Camille to return to the villa with Jerry, Paul lights a cigarette as the

camera moves in for a close-up. Piccoli brilliantly plays this moment as an opportunity for an expressiveness at once inviting and resisting interpretation. Something flaccid, passive, 'unmanly' as Camille might call it, seems to tell a pathetic story not exactly of his pushing his wife into Jerry's arms, but simply of a certain relief at being free of her for the moment so he can enjoy watching the naked actresses diving into the water. Or perhaps what he is showing is his weariness with Camille's inability to move beyond him, to circulate less obsessively, less passionately, in the world. He tells her here, as he did in the car sequence at Cinecittà, 'Vas-y! Vas-y! [Go ahead!]', an exhortation repeated several times and which may be his clumsy way of initiating other movements, other directions for both of them.

But the only certain thing about all such speculations is that they remove us from the film. All this is in our heads, not on the screen; the characters' motivations, unarticulated by them and invented by us, are a substitute for our only legitimate activity: the activity of looking and of registering what we *see*. To explore Camille's and even Paul's psychology is to play the game of the enigmatic signifier – that is, to be complicit with the anti-cinematic visuality it embodies. With our interpretations we emphasise how expressive their faces are, but expressiveness is perhaps always an exaggeration of expression, the cue for a reading there will be no reason to stop. To interpret the expressive face is to abandon the face that belongs to a visible body. Godard will, so to speak, defend himself against the threat to his visual space inherent in the very subject he has chosen for the visual space called *Contempt*. What would

non-expressive objects be like? Can a film be sufficiently lit, can a film-maker get the light right (an obsessive concern in Godard's 1981 masterpiece *Passion*) without the 'extra lighting' of the expressive? In answering these questions Godard will have saved his film from being absorbed into, and victimised by, its psychic drama.

★ ★ ★

Might there be another type of couple? Might Penelope and Odysseus be the model for a different sort of intimacy? Psychological interpretations of the ancient couple are discredited from the start by virtue of the fact that it is Prokosch who first proposes one. His theory about *The Odyssey* is that 'Penelope has been unfaithful.' When Paul tells Camille in Capri that he defends Prokosch's theory, he reformulates it with a somewhat different emphasis. '*The Odyssey* is the story of a man who loves his wife, who doesn't love him.' Earlier, in the movie-theatre in Rome, he had proposed yet another interpretation. Odysseus went off to Troy because he was sick of Penelope, and because of that he made his return voyage last as long as possible. Lang mockingly asks Camille, who is sitting next to him in this scene, if she thinks that's Paul's idea or Jerry's. Similarly, Camille's only answer to Paul's assertion that Penelope didn't love Odysseus is: 'I'm sure you don't really think that.' These various interpretive stabs come together in the more coherent if no more persuasive account Paul gives to Lang during their walk back to the villa in Capri. Now Odysseus' reluctance to return home is the result of an estrangement very much like Paul and Camille's. Odysseus had encouraged

Penelope to be nice (*aimable*) to the suitors, to let them court her and to accept their gifts. Not taking the suitors seriously as rivals, he preferred not to risk the scandal of throwing them out. But this conduct leads Penelope, 'a fundamentally simple woman', to feel contempt for Odysseus and to stop loving him. Poor Odysseus, realising too late that 'his excessive prudence' had made him lose his wife's love, concludes that the only way to win back her love is to murder the suitors.

Homeric criticism, we might say in passing, has not been entirely free of psychological interpretations of *The Odyssey*. Telemachus' 'harshness' toward his mother, his 'brusquely ungracious' manner of addressing her, have given rise to the suggestion that he suspects his mother of secretly wishing to marry one of the suitors. There has also been speculation about his own difficulties in growing to manhood 'without the correction and support of a father'. Might we not also speak of 'impulses that lurk dormant below the surface of Penelope's conscious mind', impulses prompted but not created by Athena when the goddess inspires her with a longing 'to display herself to her suitors, fan their heart,/inflame them more'?[17] Homer's work doesn't exactly contradict such conjectures, but it is also far from hospitable to them. While specific passages might appear to authorise assumptions of psychic depth, the entire epic is indifferent to them. The text of *The Odyssey* is not a psychological world. It is not the world of Euripides, and the universe in which Telemachus moves is not one that can even recognise, much less be modified by, a Hamlet-like brooding about a mother's betrayal. *The Odyssey* is the fabulous Captain Marvel comics or, closer to us, the Aegean *Star Wars* (the Wave

Wars) of Antiquity. It is above all Odysseus' wonderfully improbable adventures in the wonderfully improbable geography of his voyage. The obstacles to his returning home are the *raison d'être* of the story about his returning home. They provide the adventures of the epic, the encounters with figures and events unconstrained by the limits of realistic representation. The gods are not (or are not primarily) metaphors for human passions in Homer (as they are, say, in Euripides' *Hippolytus*); their magical powers are their most important attribute, their major contribution to Odysseus' adventures. *The Odyssey* is above all Circe, the one-eyed, man-eating giant Cyclops, the Kingdom of the Dead, the sirens, Scylla and Charybdis, the cattle of the Sun ... The appetite for fabulous stories is itself so fabulous, so excessive, that the tales of Odysseus' wanderings include not only his 'real' adventures on the Aegean Sea and in continental Greece, but also the false ones he invents disguised as a beggar on his return to Ithaca, adventures that extend his travels to Crete, Cyprus, Phoenicia and Sicily. Indeed, the actual travelling seems less important than the stories it gives rise to: Odysseus and Telemachus willingly suspend their own projects in order to listen to tales told by their hosts. If, as Paul in *Contempt* suggests, Odysseus really doesn't want to return home, it is not because of any complicated feelings about Penelope, but rather because not returning home *is The Odyssey*. Odysseus' marriage and his desire to be again with Penelope are what Henry James would have called the compositional convenience that allows what interests Homer, and us, to take place. Bereft of any significance – and especially of any psychological significance – Odysseus and Penelope as a couple provide the useful, and empty, narrative pretext thanks to which Odysseus can wander alone.

We can, then, easily agree with Lang's objection to Paul that Odysseus 'is not a modern neurotic, he was a simple, wily and fearless man'. But the relation of Lang's view of Homer's world as 'a real world' that has to be taken exactly as it is, and of *The*

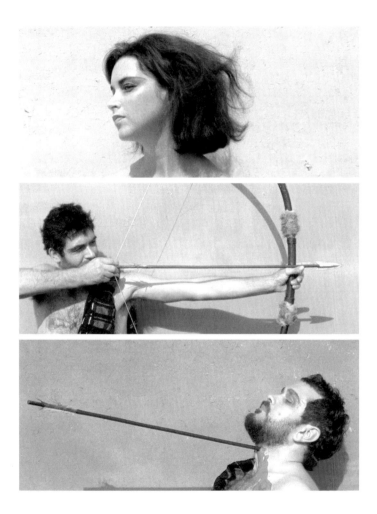

Odyssey as dramatising the struggle of individuals against circumstances and against the gods, to either the ancient epic or to Lang's own filmed version of it is much less clear. The few shots we see from Lang's film certainly don't have anything to do with either the content or the intellectual solemnity of his theories. The gods are painted plaster statues; there are a few shots of the actor playing Odysseus, and one profile shot of a heavily made-up, very young Penelope. The only action shot is of Odysseus stretching his bow and shooting an arrow that we then see implanted in another bearded man's neck, from which a stream of very red blood is flowing. The statue of Poseidon, Odysseus' enemy, returns at certain moments in the film, accompanied by Georges Delerue's dramatic music, as a kind of ominous visual mark of the doom toward which Paul and Camille's relation is inexorably moving. It's as if neither Lang nor Godard were interested in documenting their resistance to the psychologising of *The Odyssey*, in giving us at least some idea of what a presumably faithful rendering of Homer might look like. What does seem to interest Godard is the possibility of a *non-interpretive* way of relating to *The Odyssey*. In *Contempt*, this means subordinating the 'truth' about *The Odyssey* to an interest in the kind of relations we can have to it. Not what *The Odyssey* is about, but the sort of relation we establish with it when we ask what it is about. To ask about this is one way of exploring our possible modes of connecting to the past. The mode most familiar to us is one of epistemological appropriation. Even when we acknowledge the immense difficulty of knowing the past, we are always doing our best. Should we study great events and great leaders, or the ordinary lives of ordinary people? Whatever alternatives we struggle with, whatever arguments we engage in, the assumption is always that some degree of knowledge might be possible, that the (perhaps impossible) ideal would be 'to get things right'. In other words, questions of knowledge nearly always take precedence over questions about what the past *is*, about the nature of its pastness. *Contempt* brilliantly reverses this priority of epistemology over ontology.

Crucial to this reversal is what we referred to a moment ago as the film's non-interpretive relation to *The Odyssey*. In the place of an interest in the truth about either the modern couple or the ancient couple, Godard redirects our attentions to the coupling itself – not to the coupling between Camille and Paul, or between Penelope and Odysseus, but to the coupling between the two couples. This has enormous consequences for the view of time in the film (as well as of filmic time), but we might first of all note that the relation between the modern and the ancient couple in *Contempt* is but one of several alternative couplings in the film. In a 1975 interview for *Le Monde*, Godard spoke of the couple in his film *Number Two* as living 'in symbiosis with other couples that are just as fundamental: parents–children, kids–grown-ups, young women–old women, factory–house'.[18] In *Contempt*, Godard is complicitous with the destruction of Paul and Camille as a couple, not because he sees more profoundly than they do both the psychic climate and the chance events that make their separation inevitable, but rather because he has so many other views of how people and things might come together. There is, first of all, and most simply, the

58

possibility of Camille being moved from her relation to Paul to a relation with Prokosch. Even this, however, is not exactly psychically motivated: nothing (except that tactile circling of his car ...) suggests that she desires Prokosch or is even very interested in him. Rather, they are visually paired in ways that suggest some sort of immediate physical bond as well as a more mysterious bond of which they are certainly unaware. We see the spontaneous physical bond in their walking side by side in step toward Paul outside Jerry's home in Rome, and especially in the two scenes of their speeding out of the frame in Jerry's car, once in Rome and, at the end, out of the service station into a truck. Their possible coupling is from the first associated with the car, the instrument of their death. There is, finally, the image of their moving away together in the small boat that takes them back to the Villa Malaparte. This scene ends with a shot of the sea as their boat disappears into the horizon, leaving a trace of water in its wake, a shot almost exactly duplicated, except for the sign of the boat's passage, in the last image of the film. They are, then, coupled – inexactly coupled – to that which seems most alien to them: nature without people, without

place, without circumstance. This last coupling is, at most, suggestive; it doesn't tell us anything 'about' Camille and Jerry, it is simply another variation, something tried out, something that adds to the difficulty of saying where or what the couple is. There is also the statue in Paul and Camille's apartment, a silent, immobile, inanimate presence that, throughout this extended sequence of imprisoning estrangement, provides other, shifting modes of contiguity. At times the statue, positioned between Paul and Camille, decouples them; at other times it couples with one or the other human partners – with Paul when he knocks on its surface (remarking that it doesn't make the same sound all over); with Camille when, for example, standing with her head bent slightly forward, she briefly appears as a formal doubling of the statue.

A kind of doubling *manqué* is central to *Contempt*'s structure. *Contempt* the film is an inaccurate rendering of Moravia's *Il disprezzo*. The relation between Paul and Camille may or may not be a faithful rendering of the hidden sense of the relation between Odysseus and Penelope. Lang's film and Homer's epic form yet another couple, but it's impossible to say what kind of fit there is between them. And Godard's film at times films

Lang's film, but it of course includes more than what it incorporates of Lang's film. Film in *Contempt* moves in and out of an uneasy aesthetic coupling with theatre. They are in certain respects complementary partners; from other perspectives – reversible vs irreversible time, real bodies vs images of bodies, real space vs scenery space – they are aesthetic opposites. Pairing is thus shown to have centrifugal as well as centripetal energies. In the intimately conjoined couple, self-extension serves principally to reduce the desired other to a reflection of the desiring subject. Paul's love gives a seal of desirability to the images of herself Camille sees in the mirror; Camille's contempt condemns Paul to an unending search in her for the contemptible subject he has become. The lure of specularity is undoubtedly also present in centrifugal coupling, but it can be

defeated by the pleasures of inaccurate replications. The bad fit adds to both self-identificatory and complementary coupling a type of coupling compatible with heterogeneity – and heterogeneity in this mode of coupling is a non-threatening, perhaps indistinguishable supplement to a specularity it defeats by adhering to it.

The alternative coupling proposed by *Contempt* could also be defined as translation. One of the most striking aspects of the film is its linguistic heterogeneity. Several languages are spoken: French, English and, to a lesser extent, German and Italian. And they are not merely spoken: considerable time is taken to translate Jerry's English into French, Paul and Camille's French into English, Lang's German quotations (one from Hölderlin, one that is a German translation from Dante's Italian) into French, and, somewhat superfluously, the Italian directions on the set into French (*Silenzio* to *Silence*[!]). Lang compliments Francesca, who does nearly all the translating in the film, for her French rendering of the verses from Hölderlin, but her translations of Jerry's, or Lang's, English are at times conspicuously casual, or even off. When Jerry, delighted at the rushes of a nude mermaid, says, 'Fritz, that's wonderful for you and me, but do you think the public is gonna understand that?', Francesca translates, 'C'est de l'art, mais est-ce que le public comprendra?' At one point her translation comes before what it is meant to translate: 'Toutes les émotions humaines' precedes Jerry's 'All the real human emotions.' Finally, *Contempt* uses the Latin names for the Greek gods: Homer's Poseidon is referred to as Neptune, Athena becomes Minerva.

Translation is a coupling in time. Ordinarily, an original text or speech precedes the translated version of it. As its etymology indicates, translation is a carrying over, the moving of a text from one linguistic 'place' to another. It is also, as it has often been said, a betrayal: the relation between the translation and the original can never be an identity. More interesting, however, and more difficult to determine, is the mode in which the original persists, or lasts into, the translation. The idea of betrayal, after all, includes a questionable assumption: there is, or there was, an original that could be betrayed, and that remains, somewhere, as a past event. We are not arguing, absurdly, that Dante's *Divine Comedy* and Hölderlin's poetry do not exist as texts that can be read in Italian or German. We do want to suggest that, *within the translation*, there is a relation that is neither a betrayal nor an identity nor, finally, a coming after or a coming before. And this relation, which is a kind of temporality without priority, can be a model for the passionate couple's necessary (in our view) dissolution. Let's think of translation as the *opening* of the text to be translated, its removal from a supposed textual finality and its renewal as something still in the process of being made. In translations – but also in quotations, as well as in criticism – texts enter time, a time in which they can be diversely repeated without ever being wholly realised. Godard quotes inordinately in his films – through passages projected onto the screen, or through characters who recite bits of literary texts, or directly from books. Pierre Bourdieu apparently told Godard that his candidacy to the Collège de France, which Bourdieu supported, would be rejected because Godard was thought to be insufficiently literary. This is a peculiar judgment of someone we could easily think of as the most literary of film-makers. But Godard himself has spoken of 'my royal enemy, my number one enemy, the text', and he also said: 'For me, texts are death, images are life.'[19] The professors at the Collège saw something important (which should have made them embrace Godard instead of rejecting him): he destroys the text as monument. By citationally picking at literature, he demonumentalises it, therefore resurrecting it from the death of finished being, and allows it to circulate – unfinished, always being made – within the open time of film. Thanks to montage, this cinematic time can be reordered; 'physically,' Godard has said, 'you have a moment, like an object, like this ashtray. You have the present, past and future.'[20] The present, past and future as indefinite, as never having finally taken place, and never being destined to take place. In film, time's 'places' are light; they can be shifted. Film is the aesthetic medium that allows us to see the openness, the always-taking-place, which is the incorporative mode of translation and citation.

The Deleuzian and, by way of Deleuze, Bergsonian accent of these remarks should be clear. In his important work on cinema, Deleuze has defined 'the profound Bergsonism of cinema in general' as 'the open totality and the event in the course of happening'.[21] In its alternative pairings, *Contempt* proposes a non-copulative mode of pairing. With its centrifugal doublings, its use of translation and citation, its implicit reflexiveness on the nature of film, Godard's work proposes various models for a relocating of the partners in the passionate couple. We referred earlier to a critical reshifting of relational terms: from Paul and Camille as a couple, and Odysseus and Penelope as a couple, to the pairing of the two couples. Thematically, a naive question is asked in the film: what are the similarities or differences between the modern and the ancient couples? This question is, so to speak, surrounded by invitations to reformulate it in terms provided by the alternative pairings we have just looked at. The question then becomes: what kind of presence do Odysseus and Penelope – and *The Odyssey* – have in the relation between Paul and Camille – and in Godard's *Contempt?* The answer has nothing to do with likeness or unlikeness, but rather with the identical ontological status of both couples: that of possibility. The past, like the present, is always *waiting to be.* Both belong, as Deleuze writes in his discussion of Bergson, to a duration 'immanent to the whole universe'. Immanent and not imm*i*nent: neither one is about to be, both constitute a universal temporal montage in which everything, always open, communicates with everything as a phenomenon of mind or spirit.[22] History is a limitlessly extensive immanence, and this affects particular bodies (like those of Paul and Camille) as an inescapable mnemonic contiguity with other bodies (such as those of Odysseus and Penelope). They have the possibility of 'remembering' other couples in history as contemporary with them – contemporary not because of some psychic or moral congeniality, but because both are unaccomplished events.[23]

But events can of course also be accomplished, in which case they become immobilised in the subject's illusion of their uniqueness. No longer *in communication*, the modern couple

– a Paul and a Camille – become imprisoned in bodies that have lost the power both to remember and to see, become fixed in the false kind of memory that looks back at an infinitely remote, impenetrable, and improbably similar *other* couple. It is as if the unending extensibility of simple duration could, at points, settle into the realised, incarnated event. No longer circulating in an always unfinished expressiveness, the events of time have become fully expressed sediments of duration, blocks of self-contained matter. This ontological fall, or sin, is also profoundly anti-aesthetic. In their sightless gravity, Paul and Camille have lost the levity of imaginary being. In art, events *appear* to one another; words, images and sounds communicate indeterminately with one another, composing forms and structures only to play with the possibility of undoing forms and structures. Only the non-aesthetic is formally fixed and readable; a sign of the aesthetic is formal irresolution. Godard's film explicitly links the psychology of contempt to ethical issues: Paul's despair at no longer possessing Camille could lead him to a crime of passion; Camille would deprive Paul of his freedom by becoming, through the mystifying activity of her contempt, the only object of his look. But the ethical is shown to be inseparable from the aesthetic: the psychology of contempt is a crime against the communication and circulation of images in filmic montage. It would reduce appearances to being, duration to narrativisable history. To aestheticise our relation to the past is not to remove ourselves irresponsibly from it, but rather to live in proximity to it. It is to remind ourselves of our responsibility *not to be*. The passionately conjoined couple violate both the space they inhabit and each other. The world of *The Odyssey* is not, as it is for Moravia's Riccardo, a world to which we can, with comfortable hopelessness, aspire; it is a world whose permanently deferred sense we can't help but carry within us. Camille and Paul would have nothing to learn from Penelope and Odysseus, who remain, who must remain, non-interpretable; what Godard's couple might have done is to allow themselves to be seduced into the openness of the imaginary. By potentialising their relation *while they are in it*, they would have left their condemned coupledom and given to each other the freedom to reappear, always, as subjects too inconclusive, too multiple, too unfinished, ever to be totally loved.

This would define a new relation to space, and especially to the spaces of nature. The relation of the human to nature is undoubtedly the most important pairing – at once mysterious and utterly simple – in *Contempt*. How would nature appear if it were uninjured by what Lang refers to as human neurosis and which seems to be defined, if not by the film-maker Lang certainly by the film-maker Godard, as the inability to see? The final shot of *Contempt* seems to answer this question by presenting nature as pure appearance. When Godard's camera, having intersected with Lang's camera, leaves it and pans to the left of the actor playing Odysseus looking toward his homeland, Godard also leaves both *The Odyssey* and his own film. Lang has defined this sequence as the Homeric hero at last seeing Ithaca, but in *Contempt*'s final still shot there is no trace of a land that might be identified. The removal from this image of the human movements and agitations in both Godard's film and Homer's epic is emphasised by its differential replay of the earlier image of Camille and Jerry returning to the Villa Malaparte in a small boat we see speeding toward and disappearing into the horizon. Even with their disappearance, the water's foam continues to carry traces of their passage. Any such trace of a human passage is absent from the final image. All subjects – human and narrative – are left behind. Nearly everything that would allow us to measure and to distinguish is gone. The horizon line separating sea from sky is much less sharply delineated than in the Capri shot; we have nothing – which is almost everything – but the nearly uniform spectacle of blue water and sky. Just before he climbs the huge staircase leading to the roof-terrace where Lang is shooting Odysseus' approach to Ithaca, Paul passes three large light reflectors on the lower level. It is as if Godard were suggesting that for the

image we are about to see, the reflectors, used to heighten light, were no longer necessary. When subjects and objects are eliminated, the exaggerations of expressiveness lose their seductive appeal. Now everything is illuminated – not with a light projected artificially onto the scene, but rather by a light from within the elements, a light that comes toward us. We too, Godard's film perhaps ultimately suggests, might also emit light, a light hidden behind psychic darkness, blocked by our expressive being. To lose our fascinating and crippling expressiveness might be the precondition for our moving within nature, moving as appearances registering, and responding to the call of, other appearances. No longer darkened by the demand for love, we might be ready to receive something like the splendour, the 'dazzling radiance', that Homer's 'blazing-eyed Athena' casts on the humans she protects. Bypassing his contemporary literary source, Godard may have found in Homer the ethical and aesthetic solution of a perennial problem for film-makers. To be the light may be the only certain way to get the light right.

Notes

1. *Cahiers du cinéma,* no. 46, August 1963, quoted in Alain Bergala (ed.), *Jean-Luc Godard par Jean-Luc Godard,* 2 vols (Paris: Cahiers du cinéma/Editions de l'étoile, 1985/1998), vol. 1, p. 249. All translations are ours.

2. Toby Mussman, 'Notes on *Contempt*', in Mussman (ed.), *Jean-Luc Godard: A Critical Anthology* (New York: E. P. Dutton, 1968), p. 153. In their excellent book on Godard, and within a much more sophisticated critical apparatus, Kaja Silverman and Harun Farocki

speak of the film as a demonstration of how the 'definitive' can emerge from 'chance', of the cultural and more specifically textual conditions under which a contingent misunderstanding between Paul and Camille becomes an absolute estrangement – *Speaking About Godard* (New York: New York University Press, 1998), pp. 42 and 46–7.

3. When quoting dialogue from *Contempt*, we have consulted, and translated, the shot-by-shot analysis of the film published in *L'Avant-scène cinéma*, nos 412–13, May–June 1992.

4. Interview with Jean Collet, 12 September 1963, quoted in *L'Avant-scène cinéma*, p. 96.

5. *Cahiers du cinéma*, no. 46, quoted in *Godard par Godard*, vol. 1, p. 248.

6. Alberto Moravia, *Contempt*, trans. Angus Davidson (London: Prion, 1999), pp. 139 and 142.

7. Ibid., p. 190.

8. Ibid., p. 146.

9. Ibid., pp. 234–5.

10. Interview with Jean Collet, 12 September 1963, quoted in Mussman (ed.), *Jean-Luc Godard*, p. 146.

11. Another example of this disjunction between Godard's filming technique and the subject absorbing his characters can be found at the end of the apartment sequence, when Paul and Camille are seated at opposite ends of a small table, with a lamp between them. The camera moves several times during their brief dialogue from one to the other and back. But it seems curiously indifferent to their speech. When Paul begins the dialogue, he is off screen; the focus is on the lamp. The camera will begin a new tracking movement away from one of them while he or she is still speaking or is just about to speak; it will at times focus on Paul while Camille speaks and on her during

his speech. The camera also has its own rhythm: a slow tracking movement followed by a more rapid one toward the end of the exchange. It is as if Godard, in being somewhat inattentive to the content of his characters' talk, were redirecting our attention both to the rhythm of his camera's movements and to linguistic rhythms rather than linguistic sense. Finally, the use of these brief tracking movements to film a scene that might have been shot from a fixed angle encompassing both Paul and Camille, or as alternating close-ups in visual accord with each one's turn at speaking, ironically emphasises the claustrophobic nature of the entire sequence. There is movement, but it is limited, curiously mechanical in its repetitions and out of synch with the speech being recorded – as if this were the most appropriate way for the camera both to register, and to register its own distance from, the imprisoning psychic and physical space in which Camille and Paul are now moving.

12. Marcel Proust, *Swann's Way/Remembrance of Things Past*, trans. C. K. Scott Moncrieff and Terence Kilmartin (New York: Vintage Books/Random House, 1989), p. 252.

13. Is Camille also enclosing Jerry within a magical circle from which, having turned away from her when she at first offered her hand, he will from now on be unable to stop looking at her – in a manner not wholly unconnected to Penelope's (perhaps) unintentional detaining and erotic irritation of her suitors during the years of her waiting for Odysseus' return?

14. From a panel discussion at UCLA, 26 February 1968; quoted in David Sterritt (ed.), *Jean-Luc Godard: Interviews* (Jackson: University Press of Mississippi, 1998), p. 14.

15. See Leo Bersani and Ulysse Dutoit, *Arts of Impoverishment: Beckett,*

Rothko, Resnais (Cambridge, MA: Harvard University Press, 1993), pp. 173–5.

16 Gilles Deleuze, *Cinema 1: The Movement-Image*, trans. Hugh Tomlinson and Barbara Habberjam (Minneapolis: University of Minnesota Press, 1986), p. 100.

17. Bernard Knox, Introduction to Homer, *The Odyssey*, trans. Robert Fagles (New York: Penguin, 1996), pp. 52–4; and *The Odyssey*, book 18, lines 183–4.

18. *Godard par Godard,* vol. 1, p. 385.

19. The latter remark was, it's true, somewhat qualified by: 'We need both: I'm not against death.' 'Alfred Hitchcock est mort', interview in *Libération*, 2 May 1980, quoted in *Godard par Godard*, vol. 1, p. 416. For the former quote, see 'La curiosité du sujet', *Art Press*, Special Issue 4: Godard, December 1984–February 1985, p. 5.

20. Lecture at the FEMIS, 26 April 1989, in *Godard par Godard*, vol. 2, p. 242.

21. Deleuze, *Cinema 1*, p. 206.

22. Ibid., p. 17.

23. 'They had the impression', we hear in voice-over as Elena and Lennox leave their home at the end of *New Wave* (1990), 'of having already lived all that. And their words seemed to become immobilised in the traces of other words from another time … They felt tall, with above them the past, the present like identical waves of the same ocean.'

2 'Almodóvar's girls' (*All About My Mother*)

The title of Pedro Almodóvar's *All About My Mother* (1999) makes promises that can be neither easily defined nor easily fulfilled. The title in Spanish – *Todo sobre mi madre* – proposes, overambitiously we may suspect, to tell us everything there is to know about 'my mother', although we may also wonder if what we are being promised is a film entirely *about* 'my mother', one in which everything – *todo* – has her as its subject. And of course the second promise is not necessarily identical to the first: I could speak exclusively about my mother without telling you everything there is to tell about her. It is nonetheless possible that the two promises will overlap: in speaking only about my mother, I could also be telling you everything about her. The title in English is somewhat less assertive in what it promises. It does suggest that 'my mother' will be the film's subject, but it is much more casual about the exact amount of information it will give us about her. The 'all' here is less emphatic, less independent; it is part of the colloquialism 'all about', and as such it signifies totality less seriously, even somewhat carelessly. When we say 'Tell me all about your day' or 'Tell me all about your trip', we are expressing our (real or feigned) eagerness to hear about these subjects, but not at all necessarily a hunger for an exhaustive account of either 'your day' or 'your trip'. Indeed, depending both on the subject and the tone with which the request is made, 'all about' can even be ruthlessly selective. Anxious to be let in on some secret, to learn something scandalous, we demand 'Tell me all about him!' – which, far from being a request for biographical or psychic totality, is a demand for particulars, for the nitty-gritty, the very particular dirt.

But why speak at all about the English title of Almodóvar's film – a title that could simply be a faulty translation? We do so because the film suggests that something very close to the English translation may have been the original title, and that the translated title may be the Spanish title. Early in the film, Esteban (Eloy Azorín) and his mother Manuela (Cecilia Roth) are sitting on a couch having dinner and watching a dubbed version of Joseph Mankiewicz's 1950 film *All About Eve*. Esteban, whose ambition is to be a writer, and who has begun writing about his mother for a competition, complains to Manuela that the Spanish version of Mankiewicz's title – *Eva al desnudo* – is all wrong: the proper title, he claims, is *Todo sobre Eva*. Immediately after this, we see Esteban beginning to write in his notebook what will presumably be the title of the piece he has just referred to. He forms the word 'Todo', and then the title of Almodóvar's film appears on the screen for the first time, in red and white block letters, in the space between the seated Esteban and his mother.

A lot is going on here. First of all, it is not at all certain that Esteban's – and Almodóvar's? – version of the American film's title is closer to 'all about Eve' than the official Spanish translation is. Mankiewicz's title has its own share of perverseness. It suggests, casually but unambiguously, that the film's principal subject is Eve Harrington (Anne Baxter), whereas *All About Eve* is at least as much about Margo Channing (the true star role, played by Bette Davis). Insofar as the film *is* about Eve, *Eva al desnudo* captures very well the more sinister connotations of the English title. The trouble with the Spanish title is not exactly that it is wrong, but rather

that it gets those connotations too quickly. Ideally, we would go into the film taking 'all about Eve' in its neutral or benign sense (the 'Tell me all about your day' sense), and then the film would teach us to read the title as a more portentous promise: the sweet adoring fan is unmasked as a monster of envy and unscrupulous ambition. What is interesting about Esteban's not too accurate correction is that it is picked up, as it were, by Almodóvar. More exactly, Almodóvar has chosen to present his choice of his own film's title (and its possible source in the title of Mankiewicz's film) as his copying of his character's choice. The film has been without a title for its first few minutes; it is only when Esteban writes 'Todo' as the first word of his own composition that *Todo sobre mi madre* appears on the screen as the title for Almodóvar's finished film. The effect of this juxtaposition is to encourage us to identify Almodóvar with Esteban – or rather to identify the boy with a younger Almodóvar, an Almodóvar without accomplishments, with, for example, only a project for a piece of writing to be called *Todo sobre mi madre* (and not a work finished more than thirty years later in his – whose? – life, a film this time, with the same title).

The serious problem with this identification is that Almodóvar the writer and film-maker does away with Esteban a few minutes after the scene we have been discussing. The boy is run over by a car on his seventeenth birthday (after attending, with his mother, a performance of *A Streetcar Named Desire*), and what will interest us most about his mother will take place after his death. Almodóvar and Esteban have important things in common: their artistic vocation and their devotion to their mothers. (Almodóvar's mother, about whom he has spoken with great affection, appears in four of his films; she died shortly after the completion of *All About My Mother.*) To say that is to suggest, according to popular psychoanalytic wisdom, that they have something else in common: homosexuality. Remember also that, at least in English, a gay man might refer, perhaps ironically, to that 'wisdom' by saying about the origins of his homosexuality: 'Of course, it's all about my mother ...' Esteban, it's true, is not portrayed as a homosexual; he is coded as one. As if his artistic sensibility, his father's absence and his great love for his mother were not enough, his aesthetic tastes leave no doubt – for a public even minimally trained in such codes – about his gay sensibility: Bette Davis, Truman Capote and Blanche DuBois. We may begin to suspect that in plotting the death of his young double, Almodóvar is also doing away, at least aesthetically, with his – with their – homosexuality. The presumed gay sensibility does not, however, disappear. *A Streetcar Named Desire* will play a major role in the rest of the film, and Almodóvar appears to be at least as devoted to the great campy actresses, and to his mother, as Esteban is (among those to whom Almodóvar dedicates his film are actresses who play actresses – Bette Davis is one of those mentioned – and Almodóvar's mother).

There is also a dedication to men who act and become women, which could be taken as a tender joke on poor Esteban. It (more or less) describes his father, about whom the boy knows nothing. He does, however, very much want to know about his father, and Manuela promises, a moment before he is struck down running after a taxi to get an auto-graph from the actress he has just seen in the role of Blanche DuBois, to tell him all when they return home later that evening. Curiously, Esteban's 'homosexuality' is neither estab-lished nor denied; it is heavily coded, and ignored. The identification between Almodóvar and Esteban has been

made, the gay sensibility has been (and will be) embraced, but homosexuality as a sexual preference is irrelevant to both Esteban as a character in the film and, correlatively, Almodóvar's identification with him. What *is* relevant to Esteban's character is his obsessive curiosity about his father. It is as if the gay coding were put into place as the perhaps secret logic of that curiosity and, primarily, in order to be separated, liberated, from that curiosity. Esteban is insistently anguished about the paternal gap in his life, a gap that has been just as insistently maintained by Manuela. He begs her to talk to him about his father and when, much later, she finds Esteban's father in Barcelona, she shows him passages from their son's notebook in which Esteban had expressed his grief at finding photos from Manuela's youth from which half of the image had been cut away. It was, he wrote, as if half of his own life had been taken from him; to be whole, he needs that missing image, which would mean knowing about his father. Almodóvar's film may be 'all about my mother', but the story his surrogate self wants to hear would be, and he says exactly these words, 'todo sobre mi padre'.

Almodóvar tells, and refuses to tell, that story. In a sense, the entire film is a search for the father, at first on the part of Esteban, and then on the part of Manuela, who leaves Madrid for Barcelona after Esteban's death in order to find his father and tell him about his son. But the story Almodóvar has to tell about the father is a startling subversion of paternal identity. It is a story that might have seriously compromised, even while satisfying, Esteban's longing for a father, and it ultimately dismisses whatever attributes – of power, of justice, of legality

– we might 'normally' associate with the paternal function. It turns out that half of the missing half in Esteban's life is identical to the half he already knows. The young lovers Manuela and Esteban had come from Argentina to Spain. Esteban left to work in Paris, and returned to Barcelona as Lola two years later. He returned, more precisely, half-transsexualised, with his male genitals intact and with breasts larger than his wife's. It is with this partial copy of herself that Manuela conceived her son. Unhappy with her more or less newly gendered mate – not, as far as we can tell, because of his new anatomical make-up but rather because of a persistent machismo that led him/her to run after other women while forbidding Manuela to wear a mini-skirt or a bikini on the beach – Manuela had fled to Madrid early in her pregnancy without telling Lola that he/she was soon to be a mother/father.

Back in Barcelona, Manuela eventually finds Lola, although she really hasn't spent much time searching for him/her. The Barcelona sequences are about Manuela's friendships with three other women. Soon after her arrival, she takes a cab to a remote pick-up area where, in a Felliniesque scene, the cars and motorcycles of male clients circle around, and

inspect, variously gendered prostitutes (women, drag queens and transsexuals). Apparently hoping to find Lola at work here, Manuela instead runs into Agrado, a former truck driver and friend from many years ago who, like Esteban, had had an incomplete sex change in Paris that had allowed her to return to Barcelona as a prostitute specialised in oral sex. The warm, funny, generous Agrado is magnificently played by the actress Antonia San Juan, while the role of the more sombre Lola (drug user, thief, dying of AIDS) is taken by the actor Toni Cantó – casting decisions that schematise and reflect these characters' anatomical allegiances to both sexes (Agrado has also kept his/her penis). Agrado and Esteban are gender-transitions without end-points. Somewhat less sexually ambiguous is the great actress Huma Rojo (Marisa Paredes), whose autograph Esteban *fils* had been pursuing when he was killed and who is now playing Blanche in Barcelona. Huma, who is having a troubled affair with the actress who plays Stella (Candela Peña) in *Streetcar,* hires Manuela as her personal assistant, and they become friends. Finally, Manuela takes in Rosa (Penelope Cruz), a nun who, in the course of her social work with prostitutes, has been seduced by Lola and is now carrying their child. Rosa dies giving birth to Esteban Number Three who, like his parents, is HIV-positive. Manuela returns to Madrid with the baby and comes back with him two years later to Barcelona. Esteban has negativised the virus, and his case will be studied by scientists at an AIDS conference in Barcelona. In the film's final scene, Manuela happily tells all this to Agrado and Huma (the former took over Manuela's job with Huma). Huma's cocaine-addicted lover-colleague

Nina has married a man, returned to her native village, and given birth, as Agrado reports with some satisfaction, to an exceptionally ugly child. Thus the friends are reunited, and Esteban lives again.

★ ★ ★

'My films', Almodóvar has said, 'always told a story. That was my strongest desire from the first moment I held a camera.'[1] The plots of Almodóvar's films can be extraordinarily intricate – and improbable. His films are about much more than his stories, but it will be difficult to avoid plot summaries when speaking of them. So many wild plot lines are being simultaneously developed in an Almodóvar film that to summarise his stories could become a nightmarish chore. The filmography of the valuable *Conversations With Almodóvar* includes a plot summary with each film, but by the eleventh of the thirteen films the person responsible for this work seems to have given in to his or her exasperation and, for *The Flower of My Secret* (1995) and *All About My Mother*, stops the summary, without explanation, before getting half-way through the narratives. Almodóvar moves comfortably among various sorts of narrative wildness: the campy, improbable comedy of *Pepi, Luci, Bom and Other Girls on the Heap* (1980) and *Labyrinth of Passion* (1982), the melodramatic violence of *Matador* (1986), in which two lovers kill each other just as they reach the most ecstatic orgasms of their lives, the murderous jealousies of *Live Flesh* (1997), the protracted conversational rape scene *and* the serial killer protagonist of *Kika* (1993 – *Matador*, *Live Flesh* and *Kika* all have climaxes in which a man and a woman kill each other), and the somewhat unusual spirituality of *Dark Habits* (1983), with its convent run by a lesbian, coke-sniffing Mother Superior surrounded by nuns who are called Sister Manure, Sister Rat, Sister Damned and Sister Snake. The most extravagant roles are played with neither melodramatic intensity nor ironic self-consciousness, but rather with the sort of casual seriousness perhaps best exemplified by Chus Lampreave as, for example, the sensationalist novelist Sister Rat in *Dark Habits*. Almodóvar, like Godard and Alain Resnais, has 'his' actors (in Almodóvar's case, mainly actresses, referred to in Spain as 'Almodóvar's girls') who appear in several of his films. It is as if he recognised and cultivated – most notably in Lampreave, Carmen Maura, Victoria Abril, Marisa Paredes, Rossy de Palma, and Antonio Banderas – a remarkable talent for playing extravagance as if it were wholly natural without, however, in any way attempting to make it appear psychically plausible.

In Almodóvar's work, psychic implausibility does not make for narrative chaos. Part of the fun in making up these wild stories may well have been in not allowing for any loose narrative threads, in making compatible the multi-directional story with compositional tightness. And yet this exceptional talent for imaginative play – for a seemingly undisciplined indulgence in, and control of, that play – would have a somewhat limited formal interest if it were not at once motivated and countered by another register of the imaginary, one that is neither plausible nor implausible, that can, as it were, lend its pressure to either realistic or fantastic narrative. This other imaginary gives to Almodóvar's work a psychic consistency and a psychic depth, although it is also, as we shall see, inherently antagonistic to the aesthetic. This is the consistency of desire – more specifically, of sexual desire. At first, sexuality is presented as nothing more serious, and nothing more interesting, than a funny psychic anomaly. In *Labyrinth of Passion*, Sexilia (Cecilia Roth) consults a psychoanalyst in order to be cured of her nymphomania and her phobic avoidance of the sun. Intentionally or unintentionally, Almodóvar rewrites a similar coupling of sexuality and a terror of the light in Racine's Phèdre. When Phèdre flees the sun, she gives a great if monstrous dignity to her sexual passion for Hippolyte: it pollutes the universe, and in fleeing the unforgiving gaze of her solar ancestor, Phèdre's guilty desire proclaims its cosmic importance. Sexilia's phobia, on the other hand, is not the consequence of her uncontrollable desires. They are equal, both on the same level of psychic pathology, both merely weird symptoms of dysfunctional being. The other sexually obsessed figure in the film is similarly trivialised and pathologised. Sadec (Antonio Banderas in his first Almodóvar role), having had sex and fallen madly in love with Riza (Imanol Arias), son of the emperor of Tiran, can follow Riza's traces around Madrid after Riza leaves him, and finally almost catch up with him, thanks to his (Sadec's) exceptionally developed sense of smell. Thus desire performs itself as passionately sniffing nostrils, and Almodóvar once again (intentionally or unintentionally?) comically refers us to another illustrious cultural precedent: that of Freud asserting (in *Civilisation and Its Discontents* [1930]) that 'the whole of [man's] sexuality' has suffered from the depreciation, in the course of human evolution, of his sense of smell.[2]

Sexual obsession will soon become more central – and less comical – in Almodóvar's cinematic narratives. Violent death brings together the heterosexual couple of *Matador*. Both Maria Cardenal (Assumpta Sema) and the retired matador Diego Montes (Nacho Martínez) kill their sexual partners during sex; the perfect sexual act, and the perfect act of violence, will be killing each other as they reach orgasm together. *The Law of Desire* homosexualises this fantasy of sex and violence. Antonio (Antonio Banderas) becomes obsessively attached to the film director Pablo Quintero (Eusebio Poncela) after having with Pablo his first homosexual experience. Antonio kills the young man Pablo loves and, after keeping the police at bay long enough to make love once more with Pablo, he shoots himself. *The Law of Desire* both centres this obsessive sexuality and distances itself from it. The film opens with a sequence from one of Pablo's films in which a young man is being coached for a porno scene. He masturbates with his back turned to us, his buttocks raised, repeating 'Fuck me!' The words are instructions given to him by two middle-aged men directing the scene, who seem more turned on by it than the actor, who refuses to cry 'Fuck me!' until he is assured that no one will take up the invitation. Once the scene is over, he picks up his money, with a more authentic expression of pleasure, from the table next to the bed where the pseudo-action has taken place. Soon after this we see Antonio alone in a toilet stall, voicing the same request, but really turned on by the prospect of its being satisfied. Pablo accommodates him shortly thereafter in a scene whose non-pornographic realism is emphasised by Antonio's obvious discomfort as he is being penetrated for the first time. The film *moves toward* its sexual seriousness; it's as if that seriousness were anticipated, and put into question, in a version of sex as pure construction. We see it both as an unexciting construction for the porno actor and as an exciting one for Antonio in the toilet stall before sexual demand becomes the film's deadly serious subject. The suggestion of desire as artefact is made even stronger by the solipsistic nature of Pablo's love for Juan (Miguel Molina): as if he were writing a scenario for one of his films, Pablo sends himself letters in which 'Juan' tells him how much he loves him. Desire is construction, and law. The porno sequence makes the connection very clear: the two older men dictate – order – the scenario of mounting desire to the compliant (and indifferent) actor. Antonio's subsequent real excitement is just as constructed. His excited demand to be fucked, delivered to no one, and inspired by the porno sequence he has just seen, can only be addressed to his own desire; it formulates the laws of a desire he will then actualise with Pablo.

Unhappy obsessive desire returns as a dominant motif in several of Almodóvar's films subsequent to *The Law of Desire*. Women suffer from their lover's, or husband's, indifference to them in *Women on the Verge of a Nervous Breakdown* (1987), *High Heels* (1991), in which the wife kills her womanising husband, and *The Flower of My Secret*. In *Live Flesh*, it is men who desire obsessively and, this time, heterosexually. The three principal male characters all suffer from an unhappy passion. The film does end with a happy marriage and the birth of a child (it began with the birth of that child's father), although this is made possible by the violent deaths of one unhappy couple and the self-imposed exile of the man indirectly responsible for those deaths. Interestingly, the narrative is a model of intricate construction. Early in the film, a young policeman is crippled by a shot from a gun pointed in his direction by an older colleague whose wife has been his lover. The gun was held by a young man who had made his way into the apartment of a woman with whom he had recently had his first sexual experience, but who now rejects him. The young man is sent to prison, and the woman marries the crippled policeman, who becomes the star of a team of wheelchair-bound basketball players. When Victor, the young man (Liberto Rabal), is released from prison, he pursues Elena (Francesca Neri), the young policeman's wife, and has a casual affair with Clara (Angela Molina), the older policeman's wife. He promises to leave Elena alone if she will have sex once with him. Until now, she has had only oral sex with the disabled David (Javier Bardem), and the night of genital sex proves to be unforgettable … Furious upon learning all this, David threatens Victor, who reveals to him that his jealous colleague Sancho (José Sancho) had been responsible for his having been shot several years earlier. Anxious to get rid of both Victor and Sancho, David tells Sancho that his wife has been having an affair with Victor. But Clara saves Victor, and it is she who is killed by her jealous husband, who is also killed by her. The price David pays for his role in this double murder is exile to Miami, and Victor and Elena can live happily together.

The relational knot of *Live Flesh* is a paroxysm of both obsessive desire and narrative construction. Interestingly, all this concentrated passion seems to explode itself out of the frame of Almodóvar's cinematic world (at least temporarily[3]), and *All About My Mother*, made two years later, is purified of desire. The mode of purification had in fact begun to be visible several years earlier. Already in *Matador* and *The Law of Desire*, we find characters outside the circuit of desire. Angel (Antonio Banderas) in *Matador* makes explicit the imperative of desire in his inability to obey it. In attempting to be as virile as the master matador who teaches him the art of bull-fighting, Angel unsuccessfully tries to rape his young neighbour Eva (Eva Cobo). He suffers from his undeveloped sexuality (and wants to be punished for his failed rape), but his failure to conform to any recognisable sexual identity – radically unlike Diego and Maria, who live and die within the melodramatic cliché that links sex and death – also seems to be the precondition for his very special sensitivity. He can somehow see and hear all the murders being committed in the city (and this allows him to bring the police to the house where Diego and Maria are making their murderous love), and he also seems to have a connection to extra-human, cosmic phenomena. His body responds with the suggestion of a mysterious, somehow knowledgeable sympathy to the eclipse of the sun that takes place just as Diego and Maria consummate their love in death. This is, however, exceptional in Almodóvar's work; it is an alternative mode of coupling that plays a much more prominent role in *Contempt* and – spectacularly so – in *The Thin Red Line*.

More in line with possibilities that will be fully developed in *All About My Mother* is the Carmen Maura figure in *The Law of Desire*. As with Antonia San Juan in the later film, Almodóvar asked Maura to play a man 'playing' a woman. Tina, Pablo's sister, was once Tino, Pablo's brother; he had a sex change in order to please his father, with whom he was in love (and who later abandoned her). Both actresses are, we might say, asked to be women for the second time, to test what it might be like to be a woman differently, a woman who was originally a man. It's as if Almodóvar were telling them to think female identities and desires 'interrupted' by male identities and desires – a request complicated by the fact that Tina's male antecedent had a sexual passion for his father, and she, Tina, has had a 'lesbian' affair with the mother (played by the trans-sexual actress Bibi Andersen …) of the young girl Tina now takes care of. In Agrado's case, does she – did he – have any sexual desires at all? In both cases, constructed female identity emerges as an excessive femininity that simultaneously hides and theatrically exposes the construction. Most interestingly, Tina is a dissonant presence in *The Law of Desire*'s plot of wilfully violent homosexual passion. Or, rather, she renounced *that* identity in trying to satisfy her incestuous version of it, a move that has left her in an identificatory and sexual limbo where, however (at least until she falls into the trap of desire Antonio sets for her in order to have Pablo once again), she circulates – her excessive body circulates – as a deeply appealing and undefined promise.

A somewhat different version of neutralised desire is enacted in *Women on the Verge of a Nervous Breakdown*. Very early in the film we are given what might be called a technical dilution, or dispersion, of passion's intensity. Pepa (Carmen Maura) and Ivan (Fernando Guillén) are dubbing actors; we see them – separately – sitting in front of microphones dubbing a scene between Joan Crawford and Sterling Hayden from *Johnny Guitar* (1954). Ivan, much to Pepa's distress, doesn't simply sit in for the passionate utterances of others; he is Pepa's unfaithful lover. If Pepa is on the verge of a breakdown, it is because he has told her that he wants to leave her, and during much of the film she frantically tries to get in touch with him. Ivan, we also learn, is the father of another woman's son: he and Lucia (Julieta Serrano) had been lovers many years ago, and she has been confined to a psychiatric hospital since Ivan abandoned her. She regains her memory when she hears, in a film on TV, Ivan's voice saying the same words of love he had said to her twenty years earlier. What she hears, in all likelihood, is Ivan speaking someone else's role of passion. The dubbed voice replaces a voice belonging to someone else, to an actor who is himself playing passion. What brings back Lucia's memory is, then, the expression of Ivan's wholly constructed, wholly inauthentic passionate desire. Lucia can now act sane enough to be released from the hospital; she is determined to find Ivan and to kill him. In other words, she, unlike Pepa, fails to profit from the film's demonstration of passion's theatricality, its reiteratively scripted nature.

We are not explicitly told how Pepa manages to come back from the verge of *her* breakdown. After saving Ivan from being killed by Lucia, she simply says goodbye to him, refusing his invitation to have a talk over a drink. What has happened? Nothing like a direct critique of desire; instead, the experience of a more joyful theatricality. The mood of *Women on the Verge* changes with the arrival of an improbable number of visitors in Pepa's apartment: her friend Candela (Maria Barranco) – pursued by the police as a result of her having taken in, without knowing it, Shiite terrorists – Lucia, Lucia's son Carlos (Antonio Banderas) and his nagging fiancée Marisa (Rossy de Palma), the two policemen on Candela's trace, and a telephone repair-man. Pepa serves them all gazpacho spiked with sleeping pills, and in a few moments all her guests (except Lucia, who has left to find Ivan) are asleep. We have moved into farce; Pepa's apartment (which, Almodóvar has said, respects the aesthetic code of a type of comedy in which 'spaces are vast and artificial even if the people living in them are penniless'[4]) has become the stage for a production, improvised by Pepa, very different from the productions of canned passion which Pepa and Ivan the dubbing artists are asked to put on. What goes on in Pepa's apartment is gratuitous, and without 'serious' consequence. Pepa leaves just long enough to go the airport (in the same taxi that has shown up, with wonderful improbability, every time she hails one on the street) to save and to dismiss Ivan. The film ends with her return to the apartment. The unpleasant Marisa has been sleeping on a chair on the terrace; Pepa joins her, and Marisa, marvellously transformed into a relaxed and charming woman, tells Pepa that she has lost her virginity in a dream. This Immaculate Deflowering (and the magical gazpacho potion) has worked marvels on her temperament; she has, Pepa tells her, lost the unpleasant hardness of virgins. (A certain misogynistic wisdom, at once repeated and mocked here, of course attributes any such transformation to the wondrous real thing …) The unfaithful lover has been dismissed, Marisa's fiancé is asleep on the couch next to Candela, and the film ends with the camera moving away to a long shot of Pepa and Marisa sitting together on the terrace, the city behind them, continuing a conversation we can no longer hear.

In one of his conversations with Frédéric Strauss, Almodóvar remembers with affection an at once ordinary and highly suggestive scene from his childhood: that of women in his provincial village sitting together and talking. He has also said:

> This vagueness, this walking about, of the female characters [in his first feature film, *Pepi, Luci, Bom*] interests me very much. Someone who is alone, who doesn't have any particular goal and who is always close to a state of crisis, is exceptionally *available*, anything can happen to her, and she is therefore an ideal character for telling a story [c'est donc un personnage idéal pour raconter une histoire].[5]

The phrasing is somewhat ambiguous: ideal as the author of a story or as someone to tell stories about? Let's read the remark both ways; the essential point is that such women *originate stories*. Interestingly, Almodóvar has a very non-Proustian reaction to the spectacle of people speaking together, perhaps just far enough away so that he can't hear them. In Proust, such spectacles tend to set off paranoid mistrust: they must be saying something unflattering about him, or at the very least something they want to keep from him, a perhaps sinister secret. In Almodóvar's response to his ideal female character, the key word is *availability* (the person he describes is 'dans une situation de grande disponibilité'). Like that character, the women sitting together in his home town (in *The Flower of My Secret*, Leo [Marisa Paredes] participates in such a scene when she returns to her native village) are evoked as a promise. They are remembered not exactly for the experience they have already shared, but rather for the impression they give him of experience yet to be, of a prospective sociability.

★ ★ ★

What might that sociability be like? *All About My Mother* comes as close as any of Almodóvar's films to answering that question, although it does so within a motivational structure that might have stifled any such project. Manuela returns to Barcelona in order to make those photographs whole again, to put the father back in the picture in the only way now possible, which is to give him a photo of his son. In other words, she returns in order to make the *family* whole. To find the first Esteban would be to close a circle; Manuela would be returning her son to his point of origin, and with that his – their – story would be over. But of course the point of origin has already made a trip outside the family circle – to Paris – and s/he returned from that trip with the signs of a more radical crossing: transsexualised, s/he has travelled from one sex to the other, although with each new seduction of women Lola makes an at least temporary return to the Esteban still

94

appended to her body. Long before we know all that, the film has trained us to expect and to enjoy more diversified forms of travelling, of moving from one point to another. The first credits, which appear juxtaposed to medical instruments in a hospital room, are accompanied by a multi-directional feast of camera work. We move in a tracking shot from left to right

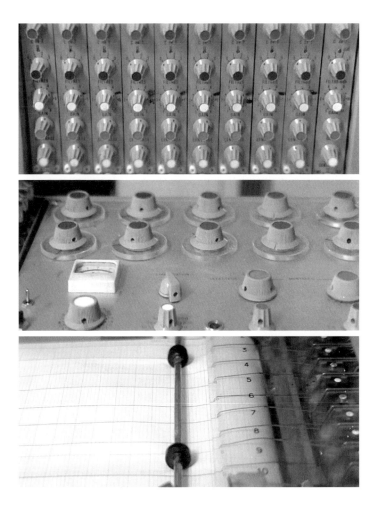

along an unidentified background of light-coloured rectangles (probably the room's windows); the shot continues in a downward vertical movement along an IV apparatus. Tanks of oxygen fade in as a new horizontal tracking shot from left to right begins. This movement ends on an objectless grey background against which 'UN FILM DE ALMODÓVAR' appears in white and red letters. The camera pauses with the appearance of each credit. A third tracking shot repeats the first one in reverse directions: at first in an upward vertical movement along a panel of brightly coloured controls, and then from right to left, and ending finally and up to a close-up of Manuela's face. She is an organ transplant co-ordinator, and we are watching the first of three organ transplant sequences (all of which take place in the first fifteen minutes of the film). A patient has just died; his liver will be given to someone else. Manuela also acts in simulations designed to train medical personnel in transplant procedures and psychology. Esteban comes to the hospital to watch his mother play the role of a woman who has just lost her husband; two male doctors attempt to get her permission to use one of his organs for a transplant. Finally, the same two doctors will, soon after, sit in front of Manuela no longer playing a role; they confirm Esteban's death to her and she signs a document authorising the use of his heart for a transplant. Almodóvar had used almost exactly the same transplant-motif sequence at the beginning of *The Flower of My Secret*, but it seems to have been only with *All About My Mother* that he was able to account for its appeal. The sequence is narratively gratuitous in the earlier film; in *All About My Mother* it is the

first of numerous transports or crossings over, the first variation on multiple cases of mobile or shifting identities. Manuela reacts to the transplant as if it gave her one more chance to see Esteban, as if he were alive in a new body. She goes to Coruña to see the man who has received Esteban's heart leave the hospital – that is, as she explains it, to follow her son's heart.

Not only will there be all sorts of movements or crossings throughout the film (from country to country, from city to city, from one sex to another, between different sons, among different mothers); the repetition of the trans-motif takes place within its first appearance. Rather than prefiguring the importance of the motif with just one version of it (the donation of Esteban's heart), Almodóvar juxtaposes three cases of the organ transplant example, and the second of the three is a theatrical rehearsal of an aspect of organ transplant procedures. Movement in *All About My Mother* will be inseparable from repetition. The points of arrest along lines or circuits of movement between places, psychic functions, or identities are not wholly heterogeneous; there is also a certain persistence or continuity within the trajectories of mobility. But it will be difficult to define both the content and mode of continuity. What exactly is repeated when a theatrical character or situation reoccurs, differently, in reality – a reality which is of course itself the aesthetic construction of Almodóvar's film? We are beginning to suspect that there may be a type of construction very different from the constructed imperatives of desire. The laws of desire conceal its imaginary nature; they can perhaps be undone only if the

being of the subjects to whom they are applied becomes uncertain. The laws of desire will collapse with the disappearance of the subjects of desire. In Almodóvar's work, repetition, far from certifying the reality of what is repeated, undermines the very category of the real (at the very least, as a category to which the imaginary might be confidently

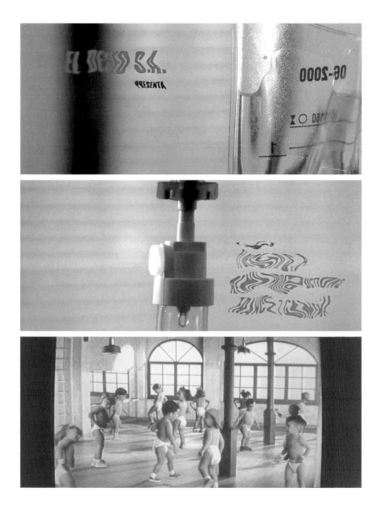

opposed). The relation between the imaginary and the real will be one of exchange, not of opposition. The remarkable beginning of *All About My Mother* announces the dissipation of the real and of the identities which the real at once shelters and constrains. That dissipation is, as it were, even decoratively performed by the liquefied script of the credits. Names and functions appear on the screen like inflated bubbles, and they disappear by slowly collapsing into themselves. Liquefaction can be contained, but it is inherently a loss of boundaries, a flowing out of frames. The first image we see is that of a plastic bag of intravenous fluid; we follow it flowing drop by drop through the IV-tubing. The containment of falling drops is, a few moments later, more humorously exemplified by the diaper ad on TV that precedes the showing of *All About Eve*: as numerous dry, diapered infants are shown exercising and jumping around, children's voices sing the reassuring message: 'Not a single drop! With Dodati you won't feel a drop.' Names as droplets, intravenous drops, drops of urine: *All About My Mother* begins with appealingly light reminders of the beauty of liquidity, its life-saving virtues, and the relative ease with which an undisciplined flowing can nonetheless be contained and absorbed.

Identities in *All About My Mother* are dissipated *as* they are being repeated. Manuela's return to Barcelona leads us to ask yet another question about the film's title: to whom does the 'my' refer, whose mother is she? She begins by taking care of Agrado, who has been beaten up by one of her tricks; she will take in Rosa and care for her during her pregnancy; her job with Huma seems to consist mainly in watching over the

drug-addicted Nina; and she will become the new Esteban's mother after Rosa's death. Manuela more or less becomes everyone's mother (including other mothers: Rosa, and to a certain extent even Rosa's mother), although it seems somewhat reductive of the richness of those relations to fit them all into a familiar maternal mould. Furthermore, the original family model is kept intact – we might even say protected – at the same time that Manuela is continuously stepping outside that model. By insisting on the first son's uniqueness, Almodóvar reveals a reluctance merely to repeat the category of 'the mother' with different figures filling in for 'my'. Manuela's grief persists. And it persists not only because young Esteban can never be simply replaced by anyone else, but also because Manuela's move into new relational modes requires a certain mourning for the relationality left behind. Lola had already wreaked havoc with the myth of unambiguous family identities, but in fleeing from him/her and in destroying his/her image on her photographs, Manuela has worked to preserve that myth. Eliminated as a presence, paternal identity and paternal prestige might be, and nearly were, permanently secured. The security is, however, threatened by the same move designed to reconfirm it: the search for the person who might fill the gap. In sobbing over the loss of her son, Manuela also grieves over the loss of the principal guardian of the paternal myth. And it is undoubtedly right that she should do so: to lose the father's absence, or the paternal function at once dependent upon and incommensurable with any real father, is to lose the Law that governs and stabilises the attributing of identities. Manuela's move outside the family circle is, most profoundly, a dismissal of legitimating symbolic systems, an implicit claim that social presence and social viability do not necessarily depend on symbolic authorisations.[6]

The symbolic cannot be *seriously* contested. The film does not, so to speak, take on the paternal phallus directly; instead, it dismisses that constitutively unlocatable fantasy product with numerous light-hearted evocations of the penis. During their dinner in front of the TV screen, Esteban, responding to his mother's joke that he should eat more because he might have to support her one day, shocks her slightly by saying: 'You don't need pounds for that, you need a big dick.' His point is confirmed by Agrado, whose credentials in this matter are impeccable: she informs Nina that 'clients like us pneumatic [with, she explains, "a pair of tits as hard as newly inflated tyres"] and well hung'. It was apparently a wise move on Agrado's part, given his/her intention of returning to Barcelona as a female prostitute, to keep his/her penis. In fact, nearly everyone is turned on by her male appendage, not exactly as an object of solemn desire, but as – what? Huma's lover Nina tries to feel Agrado's breasts and, not seeming to expect much of a response, presses her behind against Agrado's crotch. When the good-

looking and rather dim-witted Mario (who is playing Kowalski in *Streetcar*) tells her that he has been feeling tense and sweetly asks for oral sex, he also shows an interest in her penis. Agrado, somewhat exasperated by all this highly focused attention, asks Mario if men ask *him* to suck their cocks because *he* also has one … And, during the wonderful sequence in Manuela's apartment when she, Rosa, Agrado and Huma improvise a party of drinks, ice cream and talk, the general good humour builds up to hilarity on the subject of the penis. Agrado describes herself as 'a model of discretion, even when I suck a cock', to which Huma responds: 'It's been ages since I sucked one.' Rosa the pregnant nun, to the laughter of the others, cries out with mock-naughtiness 'I love the word cock – and prick!'

as she joyfully bounces on the sofa. The penis does, then, get a great deal of attention, which, far from highlighting its sexual appeal, makes it an occasion for fun. Not exactly something to be made fun of, but rather something to have fun with. Not quite neutralised, the penis is, we would prefer to say, naturalised. Unlike the absent father and the fantasmatic phallus, the Almodóvarian penis is present even where, in principle, it should not be: on the bodies of such (at least self-proclaimed) women as Agrado and Lola. The penis's many reoccurrences help to dephallicise it. Lola's penis, it's true, is at once an anomaly and a menace (she is, as Manuela says, not a person but an epidemic), but she can scarcely be said to represent phallic power and authority. And Agrado is anything but a phallic woman; she rather embodies the agreeable (as her name suggests) perspective on the penis as an attractive object of sensual and social interest, detaching it from fixed ideas of male and female identities. And it is perhaps this possibility of the penis lending itself to a non-castrating detachment that accounts for its presence as an enlivening, civilised and non-obsessive topic of interest – a passing topic of interest – at the little party Almodóvar's four women throw for themselves in Manuela's apartment.

All About My Mother invites and dismisses several serious attempts to get an identification right. Who is the real mother? Who is the real child? Who is the real woman? We are seduced into these questions mainly to be educated in the techniques by which they may be ignored. Crucial to this double enterprise are Agrado's play with the motif of authenticity and, most importantly, the movement within the film between 'reality' and art, and between stage and film. 'All I have that's real', Agrado tells Manuela, 'are my feelings and the pints of silicone' that constitute her made-in-Paris body. Authenticity is the principal motif of the monologue which, standing in front of the closed curtains, Agrado delivers to a charmed audience on the evening when, with both Nina and Huma in the hospital after a fight, the performance of *Streetcar* is called off. 'I'm very authentic,' Agrado starts by announcing, as if in deliberate contrast to the make-believe drama that will not be shown this evening. Good actors disappear within the characters they play (it is most often meant as a criticism to say that an actor always plays himself). Agrado makes herself the subject of her performance, drawing the audience's attention to nearly every part of her body. The complication is of course that this body is almost entirely surgical artifice; the part that Agrado conspicuously fails to mention, perhaps out of *pudeur*, is also the only real, or original, part: her penis. As for all the rest, it was made to order, and for a price: almond-shaped eyes 80,000 pesos, two tits 70,000 pesos each, jaw reduction 75,000 pesos, etc. .... 'It costs a lot', Agrado concludes, 'to be authentic,' adding, with a not entirely transparent logic, 'the more authentic you

are the more you resemble what you dreamed you are.' If anything is being made fun of here, it's not the wholly sympathetic Agrado's claim to authenticity, but rather the notion of authenticity itself. Agrado the construction is Agrado's dreams materialised, but her body doesn't become 'real' because it expresses those dreams. To ask if she is real or false is itself a false alternative; she is perhaps best described as intensely performative.

★ ★ ★

Agrado's monologue is a set piece; it isolates a mode of being that also circulates throughout the film. We have spoken of Manuela's grief as her mourning for a relationality she, and the film, will leave behind. But she doesn't always sob 'for real'. On the evening she substitutes for Nina in the role of Stella in *Streetcar*, the scene we are shown is the one in which Stella begins to have labour pains as she argues with Stanley over Blanche. In a modified version of the scene in Williams's text, she sobs loudly as Stanley carries her out of the house. (We continue to hear her anguished sobbing after she and Stanley leave the frame – a reminder that in a play actors don't have to produce tears; their crying is communicated by gesture and especially by sound.) Manuela–Stella's sobs are not unlike Manuela's wail of grief when she realises that Esteban is dead. One of the two doctors who have just left her son says 'Unfortunately ...' and Manuela, in a gesture whose exaggerated visibility would have been especially appropriate on a stage (where distance from the audience requires larger gestures), flings the entire upper half of her body forward and down, and breaks out crying. Film actors can of course be moved by the roles they are playing and produce their own tears, but, as we know, there are techniques for the production of cinematic tears. One of the most trustworthy signs of real emotion is, in film and in the theatre, yet another artifice. Almodóvar encourages us to remember this not only by means of the scene chosen from Williams's play, but also by the positioning of tears within a structural design: it belongs to the droplet motif initiated by the IV bottle in the film's first sequence. In more ways than one, Manuela's tears are an aesthetic construction, and yet, perhaps because it is impossible to dissociate tears from authentic feelings, we can't help but be moved by them. This double pull – at once inward, toward a grieving subject, and away from the subject, toward the producers of filmic structures and effects – is also at work (and working on us) in the brilliantly arranged close-up of Lola–Esteban crying as s/he reads the passages from his/her son's notebook in which the boy had expressed his longing to know all about his father. It is a moving scene, but while s/he cries s/he lifts her hands to his/her face, and in doing so gives us a close-up of long painted fingernails. Thus it is the

constructed Lola who moves us with the real tears of the father grieving for his lost son. Everything is real, and everything is false – which may mean that we are being asked, here and in the entire film, to construct and to accommodate a 'place' where the choice between the two, and the very formulation of such an alternative, would no longer be necessary.

Almost everything happens more than once, but not in exactly the same way each time, in *All About My Mother*. We have mentioned the three versions of organ transplant procedures at the beginning of the film, as well as the reappearance, when Manuela is asked to authorise the use of Esteban's heart for a transplant, of the two doctors who played (with Manuela as the bereaved wife) in the simulated version of a similar request. Doubling is at least as important in *All About My Mother* as it is in Godard's *Contempt*; indeed, in Almodóvar, it is deliriously omnipresent. Rosa, like Manuela eighteen years earlier, gives birth to a son (Esteban), fathered by Lola–Esteban. Manuela leaves Barcelona pregnant with Esteban and returns after his death; she will leave Barcelona again with Esteban (Rosa's son) and return, this time with Esteban, two years later. Agrado and Esteban the First double each other, although in Agrado's case

the new female seems to be dominant (she will be a prostitute for male clients), while Esteban–Lola, far from sharing Agrado's impatience with other people's interest in his/her retained penis, has clearly profited from that interest to continue seducing women. Anatomically, they both have dual identities: they announce themselves as women with their clothes, their breasts and their make-up, and, with their genitals, they repeat themselves as men.

Most interesting are the numerous communications among different art forms. One of the film's several dedications is to actresses who play actresses, and this includes not only the actresses Almodóvar mentions, but also figures from his own film. Marisa Paredes, Cecilia Roth and Candela Pena all play actresses in *All About My Mother*; Paredes repeats herself, differently, as Huma, who repeats herself as Blanche. Such repetitions place the imaginary at the heart of the film's realism: Huma playing Blanche reminds us that Huma herself is a role, that she is both the actress playing such roles as Blanche *and* a role being played by Paredes. Curiously, the scenes chosen from *All About Eve* and especially *A Streetcar Named Desire*, as well as the sequence of Huma rehearsing lines from Lorca's

Blood Wedding, assume the status of the film's narrative raw material, the already given texts which 'life' in *All About My Mother* mysteriously imitates. But it is of course not quite a question of life imitating art, but rather of art (this film) imitating, or repeating, art – although, because the film does distinguish what is meant to be real from the film, the play and the poem it inaccurately replicates, Almodóvar is in fact constructing a much more interesting comment about the tenuous nature of any such distinctions. He constructs not derivations (such as life from art) but rather exchanges within a vast realm of possibility. Long after Manuela goes to Coruña in pursuit of her son's heart, a scene from *Streetcar* is performed in which a distraught Blanche searches for what she calls her heart (which, Stella explains, is the heart-shaped case in which she keeps her jewellery). It is a curious repetition: occurring long after the episode it revives (although as part of a play written long before that episode, at once preceding it and, as a text, contemporaneous with it), and vastly different in its terms of reference (a jewel box rather than a son's transplanted organ), it nonetheless confirms the finitude and the formal unity of a linguistically designated world – a world made familiar not by inherent attributes of being but by inevitable reoccurrences within our descriptions of it.

Mostly, however, the film's terms of repetition correspond more closely. The brief sequence from *All About Eve* that we see on Manuela and Esteban's TV screen is of Eve coming into Margo's dressing room and being introduced to her; later on, Manuela, also with a concealed if very different purpose, will go backstage to Huma's dressing room. We see the final scene of *Streetcar* (closer in Almodóvar, to the film version of Williams's play than to the original theatrical text) in which Stella, carrying her child, walks out of her home, leaving Stanley and vowing never to return. It is a role Manuela had played long before, in Argentina, with Esteban as Kowalski; and, between these performances, she had left Lola–Esteban carrying the son she would give birth to and raise in Madrid. The lines from Lorca which Manuela watches Huma rehearse near the end of the film connect – almost as if they were a deferred inspiration for the earlier scene – to Esteban's death: a mother speaks of finding her son lying dead in the street, his blood flowing to the ground. The fictive doubling of the real also takes place within the real, without reference to other dramatic or filmic texts. When Manuela tells Rosa the story of her marriage to Esteban, she tells it as a story not about herself, but about a friend. With the doctor Rosa consults about her pregnancy, Manuela also momentarily doubles herself as Rosa's sister. Finally, repetition is figured more physically – as specularity – with the shots of Manuela and Huma speaking to each other in front of a mirror in the actress's dressing room.

In *Contempt*, *The Odyssey* serves as a means of derealising the story of *Contempt* itself. The film's realistic narrative deceptively presents Paul and Camille, and Odysseus and Penelope, as alternative versions of the conjugal couple. Lang and Paul speak of Homer's couple not as an imaginary construct, but as an historically real precedent to the modern couple exemplified by Paul and Camille. They disagree not about the mode of being that should be attributed to

Odysseus and Penelope, but rather about whether they were like or unlike Paul and Camille. We have argued that the film proposes an alternative reading: Odysseus and Penelope are neither ancient nor modern; rather, they *persist in time* as a permanently unsettled and unrealised possibility of coupling. They are like Paul and Camille not because they are as real as they are, but because Paul and Camille are, in an important sense, as imaginary as the ancient couple. The realism of *Contempt* is indispensable to this demonstration. It is only by at first affirming the distinction between the real and the imaginary that Godard can effectively represent his modern couple's failure to profit from the porousness of the boundaries separating the two. The film implicitly argues for the imaginary status of the so-called real – not by reducing the real (absurdly) to pure immateriality, but by making a claim for the potentiality that persists in and beyond all realised being. (Thus, in a consequence fraught with political implications, pastness is only one attribute of past events. The horrors of Nazism, for example, cannot be historically 'explained' and thereby conveniently sequestered.) The couple that Paul and Camille fail to be is, precisely, a couple that *fails to be*, one that would persist as a timeless, imaginary relation whose sense is permanently deferred. The aesthetic is the ontological drawing back, the potentialising, of Paul and Camille's unhappily realised passion.

In a curious reversal, the illusion of completed or settled being is projected onto the art incorporated into *All About My Mother*. The principal realistic narrative of the film *un*seriously repeats the art it quotes. The fascination of such works as *All*

About Eve and *A Streetcar Named Desire* most probably derives from the skill with which they, like so many other realistic plays and films, reformulate psychological fantasy as a given, irrevocably realised world. Lacan has spoken of the defensive function of desire. The fantasy-scenarios of desire are imperative constructions, made imperative by the drives that must at all costs remain hidden. Desire's scenarios are fantasmatic fortresses, and their strength depends on the finality of their plots, the strength with which they resist being potentialised. Desire presents itself not only as a law but also as a fatality. Since desire constitutively mistakes its object for its cause (this is the truth desiring fantasy hides from us), the failure of those objects to satisfy desire is interpreted as a gap or hole in the objects themselves. Lack is judged to be omnipresent: what desire lacks is also missing in the world, not as something lost but, more tragically, as something that was never, that never could be, in the world. This does not mean that objects that might satisfy the repressed drives could ever be found in the world. *Those* objects (the partial body-objects aggressively incorporated and expelled by infantile fantasies?) constitute by their very nature a rejection of the real world. To satisfy the drives we must die to the world; the 'death instinct' pursues a fantasy-ecstasy given by fantasy-objects, and in so doing it removes us from life itself. The death drive can be satisfied only by the violence that annihilates it.

If these psychic depths have entered our discourse, it is thanks, most notably, to Freud's metapsychological speculations, the identification by Melanie Klein of the very being of the human subject with fantasy-objects, and the line of reflection in Lacan that would lead him to assert not only that 'there is no sexual relation', but also, perhaps even more radically, that object-investment is something of a miracle. These are the great moments of psychoanalysis, and, as Lacan never tired of proclaiming, they have nothing to do with a supposed cure presumed to help us adapt more happily to reality. The failure to adapt – which Freud traced in *Civilisation and Its Discontents* to the incomparable *jouissance* of a self-destructive and world-destructive aggressiveness – constitutes the *psychoanalytic subject*. And it accounts for – among other things – the perennially unsatisfied (and therefore productive) nature of desire and the melancholy attached to what can only be the secondary, derived and always mis-aimed scenarios of desire. If *A Streetcar Named Desire* is such an important foil in *All About My Mother* against which the Almodóvarian world will be constructed, it is perhaps because Almodóvar recognised in Williams's play an ideally transparent version of the failures and the melancholy inherent in desire. Blanche DuBois is a glamorously pathetic caricature of the psychoanalytic subject's absence from the world.

To say this, however, is also to say that the psychoanalytic subject – and psychoanalysis – has little to say to us about possible exchanges with the world (exchanges which would be neither projections nor incorporations nor adaptive techniques). *All About My Mother* shows us such exchanges working out of, and against, desire and its fantasies. More precisely, it implicitly makes an argument for an aesthetic subject, one for whom a relationality that includes the real world (and not merely our fantasy-inscriptions on the world) is born not from a dismissal of the real but rather from an elaboration of the real as always in the process of being real-ised. By inaccurately replicating them in his own film, Almodóvar appears to be suggesting that the characters from *Streetcar* and *All About Eve* are *insufficiently aestheticised*. His many repetitions – both intertextual and intra-textual – are a way of re-initiating identities and situations rather than emphatically reconfirming them. As a result, the film becomes a massive deconstruction of its title. 'All About' is mere epistemological fantasy. There is no single (or proprietary) subject to support 'My' (Esteban? which one? Rosa? Almodóvar?) and 'Mother' has no clearly identifiable referent (Almodóvar's mother? what is the relation between the mother of the title and the mother of the dedication? can 'mother' include all the ways Manuela cares for others?). 'Mother' is both present and already lost everywhere; its presence *is* its lostness, the unlocatable and unsettled nature of its referent and its attributes. Repeatable being – being that continuously fails to be unique – creates a hospitable world of correspondences, one in which relations, no longer blocked by difference, multiply as networks of similitudes. It is as if the reappearance of identities were antecedent to their realisation; we could even say that nothing is ever even about to be because imminence is always pre-empted by the power to persist inherent in purely potential being.

Unlike the Homeric references in Godard's *Contempt*, Almodóvar's aesthetic references in *All About My Mother* are to works that are fantasmatically heavy and deficient in the imaginary. The movement in the film between these works and the diegetically defined real is nonetheless crucial to Almodóvar's elaboration of the imaginary. They serve on the one hand to make the important point that the imaginary as a mode of potentialised being is not to be restricted, and sequestered, within the category of 'art'. The retreat from being is not a particularity of the aesthetic narrowly conceived; it is an ethical duty coextensive with life itself. On the other hand, the continuous visiting of works of art provides us with a perhaps necessary renewed contact with an activity consecrated, so to speak, as the most specialised manifestation of the imaginary. The inherent immateriality of all works of art subverts the melancholy gravity of even the most fantasmatically weighted indulgence. The astonishing final shot of *All About My Mother* reasserts the necessity of this movement to and from the work of art. Manuela, Agrado and Huma have been reunited in

Huma's dressing room. The actress has to leave to go on stage; the film ends with a close-up of her face as she stands in the doorway of the dressing room looking at her friends (and directly into the camera), and she asserts, solemnly, 'I will return [Me vuelvo].' We may at first find the solemnity disconcerting, strangely inappropriate (isn't she simply saying 'I'll see you after the performance'?). And yet this remarkable moment condenses, and very nearly sacralises, the movement that has sustained the entire film. Huma, looking like a priestess in her long wig, seems to be carrying us with her to an unidentified performance which, however, we will never see, at the same time as she announces, with oracular authority, her return to the diversions of ordinary sociability.

All About My Mother is a performative reflection on the possibility of a non-fantasmatic imaginary. It proposes an answer to a question of great consequence: how might the imaginary be separated from the defensive functions of fantasy? Almodóvar's very early films light-heartedly answer this question without, as it were, taking the trouble to acknowledge its difficulty. *All About My Mother* is of necessity less exuberantly wild than *Pepi, Luci, Bom* and *Labyrinth of Passion*: the exhilarating lightness of the imaginary is, in Almodóvar's most recent film, in frictional and possibly dangerous contact with the seriousness of settled identities and established being. The threat comes from two directions: from the rigid fantasy-structures of the very works that seem to inspire Almodóvar's version, in this film, of a non-fantasmatic imaginary, and from the family structure that unravels even as Manuela awaits the meeting that might consolidate it. Much earlier in this discussion we noted the persistence of a gay sensibility in the film long after the son coded as gay has died. This was, it now seems, too rapid an identification of what remains of a homosexuality that was never, after all, entirely present. The son's death, the transsexualising of the father, and the ironic repetitions of the icons of a gay sensibility create a psychic climate in which gayness is nearly unrecognisable. And yet, having been so emphatically posited in the film's early sequences, it continues to operate in important ways. But we should perhaps no longer speak of a cultural sensibility. Our entire analysis has anatomised a more fundamental relation between the subject and the world. The dispersal and repetition of identities in the film point to a solidarity or homo-ness of being, the partial reoccurrences of all subjects *elsewhere*. Identities are never individual; homosexual desire would be the erotic expression of a homo-ness that vastly exceeds it, a reaching out toward an *other sameness*.

Almodóvar's non-fantasmatic imaginary in *All About My Mother* seems to depend on the extinction of desire, an extinction signalled by the absence of the father as the legislator of desire and the death of the (author–)son as the possible subject of desire. Homosexual desire is, however, obliquely referred to by nearly everyone's very unsolemn interest in the penis. The male organ, we have suggested, is naturalised. It is by no means excluded as an erotic object, but it has become an erotic object dephallicised and depsychologised, thereby at least raising the possibility of a gay (and straight) desire for the male body that would no longer be burdened by fantasy-illusions of power and castration. More importantly, the erasure of any relations at all between men in *All About My Mother* clears the field for an extraordinary reworking of the absence of desire for women. Far from being the more or less willing participants in a non-erotic gay sociability, women are given the space not only to reinvent themselves, but, more radically, to refashion relationality itself. Almodóvar's women, unlike those in the work of Tennessee Williams, are not fantasy-constructions of a repressed, distorted and vengeful heterosexual desire. Such elaborations are undoubtedly – however reluctant many of us may be to agree with this – *one* fate of heterosexual desire when, at least as far as conscious sexual preferences go, it has been completely occluded by homosexual desire. It is perhaps Almodóvar's desexualising and depsychologising of homosexuality that make possible a very different version of sexual indifference toward women. In a discussion of *All About My Mother* with Frédéric Strauss, Almodóvar has said: 'the fact that a group of women are speaking together constitutes the basis of fiction, the origin of all stories'.[7] But what stories will they tell? We take it as a sign of Almodóvar's generosity that he does not simply identify those fictions with his own stories *about* women. If his work suggests that he is not quite sure what those stories will be, what forms the talk will take, it may be because his talk, like everyone's talk, can't help but be inspired and nourished by our culture's richly significant narratives of desire and psychic complexity. In a new relational regime, what will there be to talk about? Almodóvarian sociability is remarkably less constrained by that richness than sociability usually is, but perhaps because he has come very close to escaping from 'the laws of desire', he is all the more anxious (eager – and a little worried?) about what exceeds them. There is, at any rate, the exhilarating freshness of that modest party in Manuela's apartment, and there is the great and touching modesty of Almodóvar himself moving his camera out of hearing range as Pepa and Marisa converse on Pepa's terrace at the end of *Women on the Verge of a Nervous Breakdown*. As if his characters were about to speak of things that he, Almodóvar, has not yet been able to imagine.

Notes

1. Frédéric Strauss, *Conversations avec Almodóvar* (Paris: Cahiers du cinéma, 2000), p. 14. These conversations were translated into French by several people. There was an earlier version of the talks that was published in English by Faber and Faber in 1996. The English translations given here are ours.

2. Sigmund Freud, *Civilisation and Its Discontents*, trans. James Strachey (New York: W. W. Norton, 1961), p. 62.

3. It would be not quite accurate to say that 'passion' returns in Almodóvar's latest film, *Talk To Her* (2002), since what would ordinarily qualify as 'love' and 'friendship' (the two men's attachment to the two women in a coma, and their developing attachment to each other) is, we feel, Almodóvar's extraordinary reimagining of the intimacies referred to by those words. The women, unable to speak, somehow 'speak' so powerfully in being spoken to that they create between the two men – as a kind of innovative refraction of the feelings directed toward them – a relation that includes them, a relation so strong, so inclusive and so new that it would be inexcusably reductive to describe it as homoerotic and, perhaps, even to appropriate it for the familiar category of friendship.

4. *Conversations avec Almodóvar*, p. 81.

5. Ibid., p. 29.

6. The possibility of *un*authorised community is extravagantly explored in Jean Genet's fiction, especially *Our Lady of the Flowers*.

7. *Conversations avec Almodóvar*, p. 164.

3 'One big soul' (*The Thin Red Line*)

Nothing is more absurd, Freud asserts in *Civilisation and Its Discontents*, than what is perhaps the most cherished biblical commandment: 'Thou shalt love thy neighbour as thyself.' This commandment, revered as 'one of the ideal demands' of civilised society, is 'really justified by the fact that nothing else runs so strongly counter to the original nature of man', which, Freud claims, dictates not that we love our neighbours, but rather that we exploit them, rob them, rape them, murder them.[1] Much of Jacques Lacan's 1959–60 seminar on *The Ethics of Psychoanalysis*, and in particular the 20 March lesson entitled 'Love of one's neighbor', is a gloss on Freud's profoundly disabused view of the moral law that enjoins us to love others. The way in which Freud confronts this commandment is, for Lacan, the very heart of *Civilisation and Its Discontents*: 'that is where he begins, where he remains throughout, and where he ends up. He talks of nothing but that.'[2]

'That' is the problem of evil. If we dismiss – as it seems to us we should – the more or less optimistic psychoanalytic theories between Freud and Lacan, theories that would make us more or less happy by way of such things as adaptation to the real and genital normalcy, then we may judge the great achievement of psychoanalysis to be its attempt to account for our inability to love others, and ourselves. The promises of adaptive balance and sexual maturity undoubtedly explain the phenomenal appeal of psychoanalysis as therapy, but its greatness may lie in its insistence on an intractable human destructiveness – a destructiveness resistant to any therapeutic endeavours whatsoever. This has little to do with sex, and we can distinguish between the practices normally identified as sex and a permanent, irreducibly destructive disposition which the great figures of psychoanalytic theory – especially Freud, Klein, Laplanche and Lacan – more or less explicitly define as sexuality. In Freud, the connection between the destructive and the sexual is most apparent in *Civilisation and Its Discontents*, which, in all likelihood, explains the appeal of that work for the Lacan of the Ethics seminar. While insisting on the nonerotic character of the aggressiveness presumably opposed to love, Freud at the same time undermines his own resolutely embraced dualism by recognising the 'extraordinarily high degree of narcissistic enjoyment' that accompanies satisfied aggression.[3] It is as if the unique pleasure afforded by various sexual acts had, in a decisively dysfunctional evolution of the human psyche, intensified and mutated into the fiercest suicidal and murderous drive. Sex becomes sexuality when the pleasure of 'losing ourselves' in sex is 'interpreted' as a sign and a promise of the ecstasy to be gained from the shattering of consciousness and the devastation of the world. There is, then, a continuity between the pleasures of sex and the even greater pleasure of a massive aggressiveness. The latter is a sexual pleasure which sex can't give, to which sex is irrelevant.

This continuity is simply and profoundly designated by

Lacan's use of the word *jouissance*. *Jouir* is the French word for coming, for having an orgasm. Lacanian *jouissance* unavoidably evokes orgasmic pleasure, but it pushes pleasure beyond itself, to the point of becoming the enemy of pleasure, that which lies 'beyond the pleasure principle'. 'My neighbor's *jouissance*,' Lacan states, 'his harmful, malignant *jouissance*, is that which poses a problem for my love' – the insurmountable problem of an ecstasy dependent (for both my neighbour and myself) on my being destroyed. *Jouissance* accompanies the 'unfathomable aggressivity' which is what I find at the heart of both the other's love for me and my love for the other – an aggressivity which, as Freud demonstrates in *Civilisation and Its Discontents*, can become even more ferociously destructive of the (internalised) other when the subject turns it against himself. To follow Freud in that text is, as Lacan claims, to conclude that 'we cannot avoid the formula that *jouissance* is evil'.[4]

With the notion of *jouissance* – in fact, already with the Freudian notion of the 'extraordinarily high degree of narcissistic enjoyment' that is at once the sadistic and masochistic benefit of 'the blindest destructive fury'[5] – psychoanalysis abandons psychology and writes what can perhaps only be the final chapter of its own history, as well as of the history of ethical philosophy. Ecstatic destructiveness is unanalysable. It can't be interpretively reduced or reformulated; individual histories are irrelevant to it, as is perhaps history *tout court*; it is not determined or fundamentally affected by gender differences or by differences of sexual preference. It is postulated as a universal property of the human psyche, something as species-specific as the human aptitude for verbal language. The immense psychological edifice of psychoanalytic theory (the stages of sexual maturation, the shapes and outcomes of the Oedipus complex, the interpretation of dreams, the analysis of symptoms, the classifications of neuroses and psychoses, the mechanisms of repression and sublimation, the illuminations and subterfuges of memory) is, from the point of view of the intractable human impulse to destroy, merely a distraction, a Pascalian *divertissement* that nourishes therapeutic commerce. In telling us that the greatest human happiness is exactly identical to the greatest human *un*happiness, psychoanalysis at once 'explains' a violence that no individual or social trans-formations could eliminate, and renders superfluous any further explanations. *Jouissance* is without psychological causa-tion; it is the final cause of our desires, the cause (in Lacanian terms) to which no object of our desires ever corresponds.

There may, however, be a 'beyond *jouissance*'. By this we do not mean that we can be 'cured' of the drive that continuously threatens individuals and civilisation, that it can somehow be done away with. Rather, just as the death drive does not elim-inate the pleasure principle in Freud, what we have in mind would not erase *jouissance* but might play to the side of it, supplement it with a pleasure at once less intense and more seductive. But the effectiveness of this other seduction depends on our moving outside the very terms that have made the articulation of *jouissance* possible. Freud opposed the destructive drive to the pleasure principle within the language of psychoanalysis. And if we consider the death drive as psychoanalysis's self-discovery – that is, the articulation of its own specificity – then it is clearly not within psychoanalysis that we can define an *other order* of pleasure. To approach sex psychoanalytically was to discover sexuality as a massively destructive drive, the revelation by and to psychoanalysis of its own originality. This sexuality is the psychoanalytic reformulation of a fundamental problem in moral philosophy, a reformulation that would by definition be impossible in the language of philosophy. The mode of investigation necessarily dictates its course and its conclusions (conclusions that in turn retroactively illuminate the nature and the limitations of the investigate mode). How, then, might the problem of evil be defined – and, to a certain extent, perhaps even resolved – through an entirely different mode of questioning, a questioning neither philosophical nor psychoanalytic?

★ ★ ★

Terrence Malick's 1998 masterpiece *The Thin Red Line* explicitly presents itself as a reflection on the presence of evil in the world. The battle for Guadalcanal – the first major Allied victory over the Japanese in World War II – is the narrative occasion for this reflection. There are several battle scenes, but they don't make for much of a story. The only narratively significant event is the refusal on the part of Captain Staros (Elias Koteas) to obey Lieutenant Colonel Tall's (Nick Nolte) order to send his men directly up the hill in an attack on the Japanese bunker at the top. Staros's disobedience – his unwillingness, as he says, to expose his men to certain slaughter by the machine guns defending the enemy's position – leads to his being relieved of his command and sent home after the hill has been taken under someone else's leadership. But this insubordination, which might of course have been rich material for a war film, is itself subordinated to what could be thought of as delivering the death blow to any example of that genre: a series of questions (both in dialogue and especially in voice-overs) about the killing of men and the destruction of nature in war. That violence is unequivocally presented as evil, and, extraordinarily for a so-called war film (especially one about World War II), there is not a single expression of patriotic sentiment in the film and there is no attempt whatsoever to provide a moral or historical justification or even explanation for the violence of war.[6] The killing, amply and brilliantly filmed, is, without qualification, presented as a massive manifestation of human evil, and the only question

130

asked about it is how it got into the world. Any historical answer to the question is simply ignored, implicitly dismissed before it might even be attempted.

The heavily weighted philosophical questions begin, in voice-over, during the first sequence of *The Thin Red Line*. The film's first image is that of a crocodile slithering from land into water to the accompaniment of one long musical chord. The questions begin with the next images (several shots of huge, sun-bathed trees), and they are asked by Private First Class Witt (Jim Caviezel) who, with a fellow soldier, is AWOL from Charlie Company, living an idyllic life (swimming, playing with the children, learning to weave) in a peaceful and happy Melanesian village. Somewhat incongruously, just before these scenes of social harmony and peace, we hear Witt asking: 'What's this war at the heart of nature? Why does nature vie with itself – the land contend with the sea? Is there an avenging power in nature? Not one power but two?'

The battle scenes, which don't begin until about forty minutes into the film (the landing on the beach and the long trek to the occupied hill are portentous enough but without violence), will eventually justify these questions – with the important difference that we don't see a war 'at the heart of nature', but rather a war brought into the heart of nature by men. Questions asked later on, again by Witt, will connect more obviously with the images of violence we will have seen by then: 'This great evil, where does it come from? How did it steal into the world?' The first sequence also includes Witt's memory (given partly in flashback) of his dying mother, a memory that includes equally grand reflections about death

and immortality. Before the flashback, his thoughts are sombre and sceptical: he was 'afraid to touch the death' he saw in his mother; he found 'nothing beautiful or uplifting about her going back to God', and he claims never to have seen the immortality people talk about. The recollection of the calm with which his mother faced death, a calm we see in the brief flashback to her death-bed, seems to allow Witt to affirm immortality, even to propose a very personal definition of it: 'I just hope I can meet [death] with the same calm she did – 'cause that's where it's hidden, the immortality I hadn't seen.'[7]

These are all very large – one might also say naive – questions and reflections. The first thing to be said about them is that while Malick's film takes them very seriously, it doesn't treat them as philosophical issues. They are crucial to the film's sense, but they have very little intellectual weight. This is partly the result of the subject asking the questions. Most of the non-commissioned soldiers in *The Thin Red Line* seem to be southerners from modest backgrounds; strikingly, none of the officers speak with that accent. The least sympathetic characters are the ones highest in the military hierarchy (the officers played by Nolte, John Travolta and George Clooney).

In *Badlands* (1973), *Days of Heaven* (1978) and *The Thin Red Line*, Malick's interest and, for the most part, his sympathy lie with the socially underprivileged: the migrant workers in *Badlands*, the criminal couple on the run in *Days of Heaven*, and the ordinary soldiers of his latest film. The most sympathetic officer in *The Thin Red Line*, Captain Staros, a lawyer in civilian

life, might, perhaps more logically, have asked the philosophical questions; instead, we hear them in Witt's drawling
southern intonations and occasionally ungrammatical sentences.
As played by Caviezel, he is an altogether remarkable presence,
but what is remarkable about him has little to do with his very
general and abstract questions (however justified they may also
be). Rather, while explicitly formulating problems addressed
by *The Thin Red Line*, they also indicate, negatively so to
speak, that the film's response will be non-discursive.
Language raises questions which, Malick's film suggests,
language may be inherently unable to answer.

The Thin Red Line's mode of response doesn't need any
more than a kind of discursive prop, or point of departure, to
realise its own specificity. Moreover, from a purely discursive
point of view, more important than the content of Witt's
questions is the preponderance of the interrogative mode
itself. The voice-overs are, for the most part, neither explicative
nor assertive; indeed, while thematically centring the film (on
the question of evil), they also foreclose the possibility of
discursive solutions. They are a way of making the entire film
the repetition of an immense question, and it is, as we shall
see, within the visualisation of that question that a certain way
not exactly of answering it, but of living in a way that exceeds
it, will be found. Furthermore, the beginning of the film prepares
us for the frequently complex relation between voice-over and
image. They don't always correspond, either in the sense of
the voice-over being 'about' the image accompanying it, or,
more significantly, in the sense of its being easily attributable.
This is especially true of the end, when the soldiers are leaving

the island of Guadalcanal. The voice we hear is that of Witt, who has been killed. It is as if he were speaking for all the other men, and also as if his being able to do so didn't depend on his being alive. In addition to this, the voice addresses a 'you', a 'you' that seems to be at once Witt's comrades and a presence internal to Witt himself (but not restricted to him). These complex final moments encapsulate the work of the entire film: the *re*working of the individual within a new relational ethic.

★ ★ ★

The easiest way to approach that ethic will be to start with the figure most obviously opposed to it: Colonel Tall. Interestingly, Nolte's character is the one about whom we know the most. He has, unlike nearly everyone else, biographical density. As he says in the voice-over during his talk with the Brigadier General played by Travolta on the ship approaching Guadalcanal early in the film, he has worked his ass off, even degraded himself for his family. Apparently, at some point he might have given a great deal 'for love's sake'; but now it's 'too late' for that. And his family includes disappointments: he sees in Captain John Gaff (John Cusack) the son he would have liked to have (his own son is a bait salesman, he scornfully confides to Gaff). Up until now, his military career has also been disappointing. He has been 'passed over', as he says, and he has lived with the constant tension of feeling that there has always been 'someone watching'. The General tells him he admires him for serving in the military at an age when most men would have already retired. Guadalcanal is his big opportunity, the war he has waited for all his life. It is, he tells John, 'my first war', and he's not going to lose the battle he has finally been given.

Nolte brilliantly plays this embodiment of pure will. It is a highly theatrical performance; with both a verbal and a facial expressiveness that depend for their effectiveness on their projective power, it is perhaps the only performance in *The Thin Red Line* that wouldn't be lost on stage. Nolte is all thrusting forward movement. Tactically, his insistence that the men charge directly up the hill counters Staros's suggestion that they first outflank the enemy by a manoeuvre to the right, through the jungle. More importantly, the push ahead – the ideal narrative pushing toward a clearly defined goal – is opposed to the film's favoured circular mobility: the shots of swirling water, the circular camera movements through tree tops, Witt's walking in circles during his last talk with Sergeant Top Welsh (Sean Penn) in a half-destroyed village hut. Closer to the temporality of film – a temporality not limited to, or constrained by, forward narrative movement – the circular mobility of *The Thin Red Line* is itself a kind of kinetic argument against the invasive movements of war. It is non-purposive, devoid of the territorial ambitions necessarily inherent in military planning.

Early in the battle for the hill, Top risks his life by running into the open field to bring back to safety a comrade he has just seen shot down by enemy gunfire. When he returns alone (the gravely wounded soldier had vehemently insisted on being left to die), Staros promises to recommend Top for the Silver Star. Far from being pleased with this recognition of his bravery, Top threatens to 'knock [Staros] right in the teeth' if the Captain goes ahead with his recommendation, and he adds: 'The whole fuckin' thing's about property.' The full evil of war is scarcely covered by the easy cynicism of this rather summary if not entirely inaccurate judgment of war (and yet: was World War II *all* about property?). It is the Colonel who inadvertently gives a *psychic* profundity to Top's cry of disgust. This is his first war, *his* war; he fights not mainly for enemy territory, but for the war itself, his most precious property. The notion of property contaminates all relationality. In *The Thin Red Line*, the 'propertising' of human relations is insistently presented in familial terms: my sons, my brothers, my wife. The film – we will see this in greater detail – treats these family metaphors ambivalently.

Much stranger, much less familiar, is the notion of war itself as something that can belong to a man, as a conflict between nations that can be seized upon as a personal property. The Colonel's unswerving loyalty to a public cause is identical to his eerie embrace of the murderous abstraction that has become his most precious private possession. Surprisingly and yet logically, the Colonel, as far as we can tell, is wholly free of any patriotic ardour. He fights, he is willing to sacrifice his and others' lives, not for the justice of a cause, or even out of a sense of the historical necessity (if not exactly justice) of the war, but in order to defend the war itself – not in order not to lose a battle, but in order not to lose his ownership of the war. The Colonel's indifference to military justice is significant in this regard. Captain Staros is a much more sympathetic figure than he is, and yet Staros is visibly shocked when the Colonel, having just told him that he is relieving him of his command (without, however, reporting his insubordination) because he, the Captain, is too 'soft', goes on to say that he is recommending him for the Silver Star and will even 'throw in' a Purple Heart (for the scratch on his face and the cuts on his hands …). The Colonel, by no means unintelligent, or even uncultivated (he quotes, in Greek, Homer's famous line about rosy-fingered dawn), knows as well as Top – perhaps knows even more profoundly, at least more viscerally – that 'the whole fuckin' thing's about property'.

The appropriation of war as a cherished personal belonging is as close as *The Thin Red Line* comes to 'answering' Witt's questions. The film is, however, more about the psychic use of war than about the origins or causes of war. Witt's questions function more as a kind of musical voice motif than as discursive formulations that might be addressed philosophically or psychoanalytically. A comparison of *The Thin Red Line* with Renoir's *Grand Illusion* (1937) – another, perhaps *the* other great anti-war film – is instructive in this respect. In one sense, although Renoir's film does not explicitly ask 'why war?', it never stops addressing that question. But it does so negatively: by showing that the experience of war ceaselessly contradicts the reasons for conducting it. The film is about two 'grand illusions': first, that this (World War I) will be the last war, and, second, that the differences war seeks to preserve really exist. Renoir's work is a massive demystification of difference. Belonging to the same social class allows for a fraternal relation between Captain de Boëldieu (Pierre Fresnay) and Captain von Rauffenstein (Eric von Stroheim) that nearly transcends the national difference that makes them, officially, enemies, while a classless camaraderie between Lieutenant Maréchal (Jean Gabin) and his men collapses – in their actions if not in their different vocabularies – the class difference between them. The most patriotic moment in the film – the singing of the French national anthem at the news of the French having just retaken Douaumont – is introduced somewhat ironically, and partially *de*nationalised, by a British (not a French) soldier requesting that the anthem be played: '"The Marseillaise", please.' And 'La Marseillaise' is sung by soldiers in women's dress, during a theatrical revue they have prepared for their fellow prisoners and their German captors. The fun the prisoners have had trying on these dresses gently mocks the gender differences otherwise so emphatically affirmed by military machismo. There is also the brief love affair between Maréchal and the German woman who shelters him and the comrade whose escape from prison has been made possible by Boeldieu's self-sacrifice. Finally, there is the impressive good will of the German soldiers who, seeing Maréchal and Rosenthal (Marcel Dalio) run across the border from Germany into Switzerland, decide not to fire at them and even wish them luck: 'Tant mieux pour eux!' All this brushing aside of difference is very touching, but it is also a particularly brutal way of emphasising the power, whatever it may be, that makes for war. Nations kill in order to preserve differences that don't exist or are easily overcome; the greatest illusion is that the absence of difference can actually make a difference.

There is, then, something of a philosophical argument implicit in Renoir's film, an argument about the failure of a demonstrable human sameness to affect the will to kill in order to maintain and legitimate difference. *The Thin Red Line* doesn't even go this far in formulating the enigma of war. Its renunciation of verbal argument is nicely illustrated by Staros's mutism in the face of the Colonel's taunting defence of war's necessary brutality. The Captain is a lawyer, as the Colonel, with furious mockery, reminds him when Staros, refusing to obey the Colonel's order, suggests that Tall would do well to have (as he, Staros, does) two witnesses (useful, one supposes, for future legal proceedings against Staros) to the insubordination incident. The man of law, defined by speech, has nothing to say except that he won't sacrifice his men to the Colonel's plan of attack. When the Colonel scornfully asks him later on just how many men he is willing to sacrifice in combat – 'one, two, twenty?' – Staros can say nothing but: 'You're right, about everything you said.' Indeed, the Colonel *is* right: within the conditions of war (accepted by virtue of Staros's very consent to be on the battlefield, to direct a group of men in battle), the Captain's humanistic defence of life is absurd. When he asks the Colonel if he has ever had anyone die in his arms (as if what? as if that might make the Colonel admit that no one

should be allowed to die in war …?), the Colonel, cruelly but perhaps justifiably, simply glares at him.

War is a great evil, and yet even the entirely sympathetic figure who asserts this through his questions about how such monstrous violence could have entered human history seems to have accepted it. Witt goes AWOL whenever he can, and yet he says that he loves Charlie Company. Even more: he fights and kills; *The Thin Red Line* is not a pacifist film. But this is not because it concedes to any degree at all the rightness, the justice, of this war. Witt appears to accept, and participate in, something judged, with no qualification whatsoever, as evil. We might almost think of Malick as saying, through his film, not only that there is no explanation for this evil but also that, given its mysterious inevitability, we might as well go along with it, agree to be part of that which, as Witt says, turns men into dogs. This would be the darkest reading imaginable of *The Thin Red Line*. It would, however, seem to be qualified by something else in Witt's speech, something presented not as a question about evil but as a stubbornly reiterated affirmation of the good. But this affirmation depends on a Manichean view of the universe: is there not one power but two, Witt asks early in the film, one responsible for good and the other for evil? When Top insists 'There is no world but this one' (the world of madness and evil), Witt answers, with tranquil assurance: 'I've seen another world.' *The Thin Red Line* appears to be inviting us to identify the world of goodness with the simple life Witt leads in the small island community when he is AWOL. It is something like a happy savage motif: the natives are innocent, pure and contented (even the children, Witt marvels, seem never to fight), and it is the 'civilised' men's war that, as we see later in the film, brings disease and discord into their lives. The Manichean vision would, then, be played out in the clash between two cultures, two moral worlds incapable of co-existing. To bring one into contact with the other is either to have the evil destroy the good, or to have the good penetrate the evil just enough to be evoked as a tantalising but essentially unreachable paradise. Witt asks: 'Why can't we reach out and touch the glory?' It is the reality of this glory, of this other world, that Top resolutely denies, even though even he may have been touched by the glory ('I still see a spark in you' is the last thing Witt tells Top).

The film also proposes, if only in passing, what might be called a subjectivised version of this vision of two worlds. Immediately after the last meeting between Top and Witt, we hear Top's voice, accompanying the image of him walking through the camp, suggesting a mysterious interpretive difference at the basis of the opposition between good and evil. One man looks at a dying bird and sees only pain and death; another, looking at the same scene of death, sees glory. So perhaps the entire moral opposition may be purely a question of perspective, of a difference of moral temperaments. It would be reading the world as evil that brings evil into the world. Thus Witt's final words – 'all things shinin'' – words that nearly the entire film contradicts, would be justified by the perspectivism of moral vision. Even soaked in blood, the world, for those looking at it from within the glory, can be celebrated as beautiful and good.

★ ★ ★

This reading of *The Thin Red Line* misses its originality and greatness. The film proposes something quite different, something that does not exactly answer Witt's questions and yet takes them all into account. It is difficult to account discursively for this taking into account, since it is itself not a discursive event. The film's verbal questions are responded to visually. Or, more exactly, questions *about* the world are coupled with different ways of *looking at* the world. This is the film's principal (but by no means only) coupling. Coupling – which, as we will see in greater detail, is the film's major conjunctive mode – is neither an opposition (as are good and evil) nor is it sequential (like an answer than follows and obviates further need for the question). Rather, the looking is simultaneous with the asking; they are juxtaposed modes of reacting to the world. Juxtaposed, but not equal in value: the film enacts the image's superior inclusiveness over the word. Looking at the world doesn't erase questions about the world, but it does inaccurately replicate those questions as a viable relation to the world.

In our discussion of Godard's *Contempt*, we quoted Deleuze's remark about Bergman's use of the close-up in *Persona*: 'The close-up has ... pushed the face into regions no longer ruled by individuation.' This observation would be just as relevant to *The Thin Red Line* as it is to *Persona*, but in an entirely different way. Bergman films 'the fear of the face confronting its own nothingness'; the close-up exposes 'the nihilism of the face'. Nothing could be more different from the function of Malick's close-ups[8] in *The Thin Red Line,* even though

Malick's close-ups generally confirm Deleuze's sense of the psychologically non-expressive nature of the close-up. What we see in the face is not, however, its nothingness, but rather a certain mode of registering the world. Malick's faces presuppose, on the part of the film-maker, a profound reflection on, *and* a modification of, the way the camera registers the world. A naive but useful preliminary description of what a movie camera does would be to say that it registers a part of the world and projects what it registers onto a screen where we, as spectators, can share the protected vision enjoyed by the camera. The first qualification of this description would be to point out that the camera frames a particular vision; it subjectivises its registering (a word with strongly *ob*jective connotations) by such things as the distance it takes from objects, angles of vision, use of filters and colour, and the way it moves. The camera's mobility in particular exposes it as a moving presence within the world it films, not an immobile eye with the privilege of seeing the world from some superior 'outside' position. But this very implication in what it registers not only deprives the camera of any presumed objectivity; it also means that what the spectator may think of as the passive object of his seeing is actually looking at him. The voyeuristic enjoyment of being 'let in on' a world the camera has generously made available to our protected vision is naively unreflective; we are in reality confronted, looked at, by a point of view, a world already interpreted. And we are in turn interpreted, identified, by that interpretation. The camera's point of view on the world it films necessarily includes assumptions about the spectators of that world. Those who will watch the film have, in a sense, already been created by it. That's how the camera looks at us: it imposes on our looking an identity already invented for us.

Malick's camera uses the close-up as a way of giving a face to the particularities of its own point of view. It shows the imprint of the act of looking on the subject of the looking. Very often the close-up is unaccompanied by speech; we see the filmed subject merely looking. Characters thus become multiple cameras within the film, cameras whose points of view, however, are not mediated by (the organisation of) the objects they are 'filming', but are rather directly visible on the registering instrument itself, on the face. This gives to the faces of *The Thin Red Line* a unique kind of expressiveness. While they do communicate some easily identifiable feelings (Staros's compassion, Top's disgust as he listens to the new Captain's familial-military jargon), they are not primarily psychologically expressive. They are strongly individuated, but not on the basis of personality; rather, they individuate the different worlds we see them registering. Interestingly, the most psychologically expressive face in the film is the Colonel's; we easily read on his contorted features his frustration and rage. And, more than anyone else in the film, he *acts*. He is, as we have said, Nolte displaying his great talent as an actor, and his pushing forward is all action. Unlike the others, and except for the brief scene after the battle for the hill is won where we see him seated, and silent, allowing himself, for just one moment, to exhale deeply (as if to return the energy he has wilfully appropriated from the world), he doesn't register the world, he invades it. For the others, it is as if Malick were giving us an impressive range not of what we usually think of as characters, but rather of ways of filming – and creating? – different worlds. It is the voice-overs that carry the weight of the film's emotional and intellectual expressivity. This allows Malick to give us the face as pure visuality, almost to make, within the sound and images of *The Thin Red Line*, another film, a silent film. But unlike the often frantic straining toward expressiveness characteristic of faces in silent films (a striving toward a visual equivalent of the accompanying written texts in those films), the silence of Malick's faces clears the facial field, so to speak, for the deployment of the world their features are recording. Thus the soldiers in Malick's 'war film' are individuated not as personalities but as perspectives on the world. This sort of individuation and psychic individuality are, inherently, mutually exclusive. Malick of course shows us the world his characters are registering. But their faces also independently manifest their perspective on the world; their world is inscribed on their faces. It is as if, in order to see how objects are being registered by the camera, we had only to look directly at the camera. The human subjects of *The Thin Red Line* are, then, sharply differentiated – although we shall also have to recognise that the most powerfully individuated perspective on the world in the film is also an erasure of perspective itself.

★ ★ ★

The film's visual formulation of both the presence of evil and the possibility of a viable response to it is discursively supplemented both in the voice-overs and in a specific dialogic structure. If the philosophical content of the discourse is schematic and relatively unsophisticated, it does provide a familiar frame, or support, for a visual relationality that, in its most original aspect, has no 'argument' at all to make. The film is punctuated by three meetings between Witt and Top. Although there is clearly a deep bond between them, they provide the major confrontation in the film concerning the possibility of something other in the world than evil. Top's is the darkest point of view in the film. There is, he asserts, no world but this one, a world of madness and evil where wars are fought for property and those in charge 'want you dead or in their lie'. Since to be killed in the war would be to die for nothing, a man can only look out for himself and hope to reach the 'bliss' of no longer feeling anything at all. Protect

your unconnectedness: Top's ethical stand might be reduced to that. His sombre intelligence could easily be thought of as carrying the film's moral commentary on the horrors of war. Nothing in the film actually puts into question the validity of his point of view, and the fact that he himself occasionally contradicts his wilful affective numbness makes him immensely appealing. He is both irreproachably lucid and yet not entirely circumscribed by his lucidity. He risks his life to save another soldier, and Witt rightly sees that Top cares for him. That care is the 'spark' that, all the darkness notwithstanding, Witt says he can still see in him. Heartbroken by Witt's death, Top, kneeling at Witt's grave, turns the remark against his friend with the question, at once cruel and tender: 'Where's your spark now?'

Top is complex yet intelligible. His appeal is surely linked to that: he suffers, he is torn, the inhumanity of war pushes him to close himself to all human contacts, and yet he cares, perhaps even loves ... Although this complexity is magnificently embodied in Sean Penn's performance, Top's function in the film is more interesting than his implied psychic richness. He has the *relational* function of putting into relief Witt's *un*intelligibility. And that can best be approached in terms of how Top films the world. He and Witt could be thought of as two different cameras: one with its aperture wide open as it moves within its field of vision, the other with its aperture continuously about to close, at least to narrow the visual field. In addition to its other virtues, Penn's acting is at times a masterpiece of squinting. His response to what he has seen is to try to see less. He defensively lowers his optical shutters as if to monitor the evil coming in, and, as we see in his attempt at self-control at Witt's grave, he would also control the signs of pain, the tears, in his response to that evil. Top's eyes are most open when he talks to Witt; his disgust at the new Captain's speech at the end of the film makes of his face a nearly eyeless mask. It might be tempting to think of Top as the one who has seen everything, in contrast to a certain blindness on the part of Witt, a blindness that would account for his being able to speak of seeing a 'glory' where there is none. In their verbal confrontations, it would seem that the wisely cynical Top has the upper hand (in their second meeting, Witt even remains silent). He has seen the world as it is, and he is trying to save Witt from a dangerous naiveté. But, from a visual point of view, that wisdom is put into question: how

much can he really have seen with his tensed, at times even half-closed eyes? Could Witt's insistence on the existence of another world be a function of the remarkable clarity and openness of his look? If that were the case, then his only mistake would be to speak of the glory as *elsewhere*; he has, perhaps, seen it *here*. It would be Top who, while denying the existence of another world, implicitly believes in one: where, after all, in this world of madness, could his own goodness – or that of Witt – find its place? Nothing here nourishes it; its source is invisible, belonging to a world he at once manifests and to which he is blind.

It is this implicit Manicheanism that the film 'argues' against. The argument is largely visual, and we can best approach its terms and logic by noting some of the curious reoccurrences, or near doublings, in the film. Top's mode of looking is (a little inaccurately) replicated by the way Gaff looks at Colonel Tall while the latter confesses his past frustrations to him and calls him the worthy son he has never had. Gaff watches this cruel, wilful, pathetic, imploring performance with tensed eyes, with a look that darts rapidly from side to side – as if the crazy mobility of the Colonel's discourse were best represented, and resisted, by the self-protective narrowing and rapid movements of Gaff's eyes. And just as this look repeats and relocates the guarded looks of Top, looks that would also keep something evil or repellent at bay, the openness of Witt's look reoccurs, in a curiously exaggerated form, in Fife's (Adrien Brody) wide-eyed terror. It is as if he too saw everything, but in spite of himself; the all-inclusiveness of *his* look is a curse rather than a sign of the acceptance of all appearances.

The Thin Red Line, like *Contempt* and *All About My Mother*, contains several couplings. In Malick's film, coupling testifies to a connectedness opposed not only to Top's wilful isolation but also to Witt's description of the 'glory' he has seen as belonging to another world. These couplings, which are both visual and verbal, generally take the form of reoccurrence; similitude links the two terms of most of these couples. Not only is Top visually repeated in Gaff's look; what he says to Witt early in the film about the hierarchy of authority in Charlie Company is, curiously, picked up in an unpleasantly extended family metaphor by the new Captain addressing his men near the film's end. Also, in that early scene, Witt, having been caught AWOL, is in the military ship's brig where Top tells him that he has worked a deal that will keep Witt from being court-martialled. A coarser, more cynical version of this deal takes place later when the Colonel not only saves Staros from being punished for his refusal to obey the senior officer's orders, but even announces his intention to recommend the Captain for the Silver Star and the Purple Heart. A screaming Japanese prisoner surrounded by his American captors prefigures the immeasurably calmer Witt surrounded suddenly

by Japanese soldiers in the later scene that ends with Witt's death. The one example of an exclusive romantic attachment in the film is Jack Bell's (Ben Chaplin) love for his wife. And it is Bell who, as it were, is cruelly compelled by Malick to watch the scene of a sobbing Japanese prisoner embracing and cradling the head of his dead comrade (and lover?). (This scene also anticipates Bell's loss of his wife.) Even such things as the casual visual coupling of vertical bayonets and trees, or that of the triangular-shaped crocodile entering the water (from left to right) with the image of the similarly shaped Navy ship, a few moments later, moving on the water from left to right, contribute to this network of verbal and visual correspondences. Finally, there are the large structural and thematic couplings – largely frictional couplings[9] – between the image and the voice-over, (Witt's) verbal questioning and (the Colonel's) verbal assertiveness, the spark of 'glory' and the flames of war, contemplation and action.

Perhaps the principal effect of these verbal repetitions, visual near-replications and structural couplings is to represent the ontological implausibility of individuality. In spite of the important differences between them, the Colonel and Top make the major arguments for individuality in the film. The Colonel 'attacks' the war itself in order to make it a property of his ego. Only by 'owning' this massive conflict will he be able to defeat the hostile watching by which he has always been victimised. Unable to think of himself as extending beyond the boundaries of his ego and his body, he logically, if paranoiacally, imagines himself as an easily locatable (because securely bounded) target of all the looks searching for his mistakes and his weakness. The securely bounded self is the self most easily watched, and therefore most vulnerable to attack. Top's retreat into a blissfully numb selfhood is more complicated in that he can't help leaving that shell, exceeding himself in his at times life-risking sympathy for his comrades and especially in his involuntary yet inescapable sharing with Witt of the 'glory' he emphatically denies having ever seen. Individuality is a wilful non-connectedness that violates the continuities of being that Witt affirms when he speaks of 'one big self' in the universe, of everyone being part of the same soul.

The oneness that Malick also affirms is, however, considerably more elusive than Witt's verbal formulation of it. Malick takes great care to indicate what does *not* constitute that oneness. The trap is that the society responsible for the evil of war also puts great value on connectedness – specifically, on various kinds of community. The community dismissed most summarily in *The Thin Red Line* is, ironically, the one without which war would presumably be impossible. There is, we have noted, not a single patriotic utterance or reference to the Allied cause in the entire film. The reasons for taking part in the war may of course vary (they might, for example, be notably different for the draftee and the career officers), but no one seems to have any sense at all of belonging to a national community, or the moral community of all the nations joined together in the struggle against the Axis powers. Nothing could be more dismissive of the reality and the value of any such community than the film's implicit assumption that, in life-threatening battles, such allegiances are intrinsically too weak to survive. Too weak to survive not only in the men of Top's and Staros's integrity, but also for such men as Colonel Tall and the Brigadier General, who waste no time mouthing patriotic jargon and speak openly of their military lives in terms of personal ambition and power.

The community that the film does take the time to dismiss, quite insistently, is the community based on family ties, and on the heterosexual intimacy at the basis of those ties. The only bad performance in the film is Clooney's in his brief appearance as Charlie Company's new commander–father. His address to his men, in which he defines himself as the father and Top as the mother of their large family, is wholly unpersuasive. Not only does his handsome, neat-featured, unblemished face seem like an insult to the weary, melancholic faces of the men listening to him; it is as if Clooney himself (or the officer he is playing?) could hardly do more than mechanically recite the few embarrassing lines that constitute his entire role in the film. The cheery flatness of his voice is further emphasised by its being interrupted, in voice-over, by Top's vividly dark commentary: 'They want you dead, or in their lie.' Colonel Tall's sentimental embrace of Gaff as the son worthy of him is obviously more sincere, but it is set against the Colonel's indifference to his men's lives as well as Gaff's unresponsiveness (he simply ignores the appeal and makes a much more decent plea for water to be sent up to the men). Finally, there is Bell's love for his wife. The flashbacks to their time together show her as lovely and loving, and Bell confesses his lack of desire for any other woman and speaks to her, in voice-over, as being one with him ('I can't tell you from me. ... I drink you'). That illusion of oneness is brutally destroyed by the letter in which she writes that, having fallen in love with another military man, she wants a divorce. The blow is made even worse by the cruelty of her asking Bell to help her to leave him … Bell's wife is (except for the brief shots of Witt's mother and sister) the only woman in *The Thin Red Line*, and the considerable time devoted to their happy past underlines the brutality of the break-up and, in retrospect, the unreliable nature of the intimacy. If some sort of community survives the disconnectedness of men killing each other in war, it will not be the community evoked by 'my sons' or 'my spouse', communities shattered by an intrinsic if involuntary inauthenticity. '*My* son' and '*my* wife' come dangerously close to '*my* war'; 'the whole fuckin' thing's about property' may refer to much more than war.

And yet the family reference is not entirely discredited. The scene in which Captain Staros, taking leave of his men, tells them that they have been like sons to him, and they thank him for keeping them together, is deeply moving. 'You *are* my sons, my dear sons', we hear in voice-over as Staros leaves Guadalcanal; 'you'll live inside me now, I'll carry you wherever I go'. The appeals to family ties are presented uncritically only when they are meant to describe – and to describe only partially – a community of comradely care and friendship. Part of what we hear Witt say in the final voice-over identifies 'brother' with 'friend': 'Where was it that we were together? Who were you that I lived with, walked with? – the brother, the friend.' Is it, then, friendship – more specifically here, the fraternal bonds between men in war – that constitutes the 'other world', the one in which Witt has seen the 'glory'? Friendship, however, doesn't seem adequate to describe the real community Witt is taken away from at the beginning of the film, the community we might think of him as referring to when, shortly after being brought back to the military ship, he first tells Top of having seen another world. (Later, walking through a Melanesian village into which war has brought disease and conflict, Witt speaks of a family, once united, now turned against itself.) And yet, in that passage from the final voice-over, it isn't a question of the happy native village; 'the brother, the friend' must be his fellow soldiers. But, curiously, he evokes those brothers, those friends, in a question ('who were you that I lived with?') – as if he were unsure of their identity. Not only that: speaking from beyond the grave, he appears no longer even to know where they were all together. A very simple matter – his bonds with the men he has fought with – becomes a question, as if it were as much a mystery as the metaphysical puzzle about the origin of evil. And it perhaps does become a puzzle by virtue of the fact that the speaker is no longer alive, so that the questions about who his brothers were, and where they were together, presuppose prior, truly unanswerable questions about who *Witt* is now (to whom does his voice belong? how can it 'belong'?) and where Witt is now.

Such questions don't make much sense; more surprisingly, it may be senseless to ask 'who' Witt is at any point in *The Thin Red Line*. He is, it's true, not entirely undefined as a person: we know about the impression his mother's death made on him as a boy, we know that he has been AWOL more than once, that he is deeply troubled by the destructiveness of war, and that, as he says, he loves Charlie Company. But, as even this brief sketch suggests, he is somewhat incoherent as a person. He apparently flees from his military service whenever he can, and yet not only does he not refuse to enter combat, he also volunteers for dangerous missions, missions that involve a readiness to kill. He is reflective, he engages in some lofty metaphysical speculation, but he can also be defiantly macho, and ordinary, as when he tells Top that he can take anything the Sergeant may dish out to him, that he is twice the man Top is.

★ ★ ★

None of this, including the incoherence, is very exceptional, and yet it is Witt who not only poses the moral dilemma that war raises but also embodies what may be the closest thing to a resolution of them. 'Resolution', however, is not quite the correct word, at least not to the extent that it suggests some sort of solving of, or answer to, the problem of evil. In *The Thin Red Line*, the verbal questioning that reoccurs throughout the film, questioning to which nothing in the film even begins to give an answer, is juxtaposed to, is confronted by, a presence that may have the power to silence it. And this presence is pre-eminently a certain kind of look. In his language, Witt responds to the world with questions about the hidden agency of evil and claims of having seen another, better world; in his look, Witt simply connects to the world through what might seem like a distancing from it: an evenness of witnessing. His look is the most haunting presence in the film, but it is not expressive, as Top's is. Scenes of deceit and horror don't make him begin to close his eyes, to squint, as Top does, in order to hold such things at bay, ideally, to shut them out. Witt's look might almost be judged as insensitive: he watches men die with the same undisturbed look that he brings to the people of the village where he is happy, or to the leaves which, at one moment, we see him watering (as if they had become as thirsty as his water-deprived comrades). Witt's eyes witness the violence of war much as Malick shows us nature witnessing it. All the shots of sunlight streaming down through the branches of trees, of mountains in the distance just as the sun begins to penetrate the morning mist, of birds poised on a branch, of circling eddies of water: all these images, on the whole images of calm beauty (not of the unceasing strife the Colonel claims to see in nature), represent the vast, non-human setting of *The Thin Red Line* as a mostly immobile, indifferent witness to the human agitations within it.

Extraordinarily, Witt's face communicates witnessing as a mode of implication, of connectedness. His looking is a form of participation – as, for example, when his features relax, and we see the beginning of a smile on his face, when the physical agony of the Sergeant played by Woody Harrelson gives way to the quiet of death. Faced with that death, Witt fails to register the

more common expression of suffering caused by a loss. *That* expression – the sign of grief and sympathy, of deep feeling – is our way of reacting to death as a spectacle: it moves us, but it is happening somewhere else, to someone who may be precious to us but whose difference from us death confirms. Witt's 'unfeeling' reaction – the trace of a smile – is a look that takes in what it sees, that abolishes distance. More generally, it is an illusion, *The Thin Red Line* suggests, to think that we can look at nature the way it appears to look at us: as a spectacle distinct from the looking. That appearance is eerily represented in the sequence preceding Witt's death by the shots of an owl sitting in a tree, looking. The owl is indeed a spectator of the terror and the imminent violence below and around it. It sits and merely looks at that in which it is not implicated, somewhat as theatre-goers might sit in their seats and watch, from a distance, the drama being performed on stage. *The Thin Red Line* is profoundly anti-theatrical in that it not only implicitly criticises Colonel Tall's wilfully projective and stagy performance of himself, but also uses the medium of film to forestall *any* relation to the world as mere spectacle. The uniquely filmic device of the close-up – and, in particular, the close-ups of Witt's looking –

defines a cinematic aesthetic, *and* ethic, of implicated witnessing, of a witnessing identical to total absorption.

Malick is not sending us the trite (if true) message that war violates nature's beauty. Rather, the war is the occasion for a demonstration of a universal relationality of which the violation is only a part. (One concrete representation of that relationality is the image of soldiers running up the hill in the high grass; the camera moves with them in and through the grass and weeds, so that we can't help but see the men, at least in part, as another vertical element in the natural landscape.) It is within the relatedness that the violation occurs, not as an attack on something essentially distinct from our own being. Similarly, it is suggested, especially through Witt's tending the Japanese prisoners whose defeat he has also just helped to bring about, that the 'enemy' is no more distinct from him than his own comrades, although the combat against them is also part of the world as it is given and as it is to be absorbed.

Through Witt's look, *The Thin Red Line* films an inherently unrealisable ideal of film itself. A myth in film history, as in the history of photography, is that those media can give us the world as it is, that they can operate as pure recording instruments. Unlike the camera, which is always selective, always vehicles a point of view, Witt's look appears to do nothing but receptively register whatever it sees. Obviously, this does not eliminate an angle of vision, but Witt's is a non-projective angle of vision, one that fails to impose an identity on the world. Significantly, there is no indication that Witt shares Top's characterisation of the war, of 'the whole fuckin' thing', as being 'about property', and he *receives*

the images of war more easily than Top does. It could of course be objected that his description of the war as evil is more heavily interpretive than the assignment of a property motive to the agents of war. But the discourse on the evil of war is relegated to the voice-overs; when we *see* Witt speaking, he evokes the 'other world' he has seen, or the 'spark' from that other world that he sees in Top. The images of Witt are more inclusive than the voice-overs; they embody a relation to the world that appears already to have taken the discourse on evil into account. Malick's nearly obsessive filming of Witt's face could be thought of as the camera's envy of the human eye. The latter is more anarchic than the camera: if it naturally can't help but select what it sees, it also wanders more easily: it is much less burdened than the camera by the weight of a material positioning. The voice-overs question the moral being of the world; Witt's look indiscriminately registers the world's appearances. The circular mobility of Malick's camera, as well as the visual discontinuities that break up the narrative line of battle (for example, with 'unrelated' images of nature), could be thought of as Malick's imitation of Witt's mode of filming, his attempt to avoid projecting a moral or aesthetic identity on the world he films, to allow his camera to be as mildly but thoroughly invaded by objects as Witt's eyes are.

That anarchic receptivity on the part of the film-maker is of course calculated. Witt is Malick's fiction of a look that might see nothing but the world's visibility. And by so insistently presenting us with that look, and by his own willed collaboration with it in his filming technique, Malick encour-

ages *us* to collaborate with Witt's look. We see the objects and
the people Witt looks at, but in the close-ups what we see is
Witt looking at us. His look, however, lacks the aggressive
intention of Godard's filmed camera when it turns toward
and on us at the end of *Contempt*'s title sequence. Godard
shocks us out of our illusion of a safe invisibility by making it
seem as if we too could be absorbed into the camera's eye – a
trick by which the film-maker reminds us that he knows we
are there, and that the images we are about to see will include
an (unspoken) intentionality directed at us. Witt's look, on
the other hand, receives us in the same way it receives the rest
of the world. We are, as a result, tacitly summoned to be the
world as Witt sees it, and since that world is inseparable from
Witt's look, we are also being called upon to share Witt's
looking, to adopt his subjectivity in looking at the world. The
immense yet beneficent demand being made on us is that we
both be the world as Witt, looking at us, receives it, and that
we imitate that receptivity (as Malick does in the way he films
everything, including the receptive figure himself [Witt] who
is the model for his filming technique) when we leave the film
and turn again to the world outside it. In extremely complex
fashion, the close-up in *The Thin Red Line* transmits a relational
lesson of great simplicity, one that appears to ask us to do
little more than *to let the world be.*

The demand being made on us is nonetheless a radical one.
We should correct our allusion, a moment ago, to Witt's subjectivity: the precondition of his wholly receptive gaze is a subject
divested of subjectivity. The astonishing unprotectedness of
Witt's look designates a subject without claims on the world,

who owns nothing (not even the life he so freely gives at the end). Witt approaches the limit of a subject without selfhood, ideally an anonymous subject. Witt acts, it's true, and his actions delineate a certain individuality: he goes AWOL but he loves Charlie Company, and he volunteers for dangerous missions. But we remember him not for this but for his willingness *not to be – in order to be the world he never refuses to absorb*. That is, his unforgettable presence is the result of his ontological passivity – not the passivity of someone who submits to the will of others, but the active passivity of someone who, acknowledging that he *is* the world in which he lives, makes his self superfluous in order to multiply his being. The attentive way in which Witt's look simply lets the world be also replicates the world as an accretion to a consciousness, and a look, ceaselessly receptive to the world. The forms it absorbs constitute the identity of the absorbing consciousness. Lessness is the condition of allness.

★ ★ ★

Malick's film moves toward a generalising of that possibility – that is, toward a community grounded in anonymity and held together by an absence of both individuality and leadership. (Historically, communities whose members have been required to renounce their individuality have done so in the service of a powerfully individualised leader. The leader is the surrogate self, the master self, and in him the community he at once tyrannises and claims to protect have sacrificed their egos in order to hyperbolise ego-power.[10]) This possibility is raised quite early in the film, and it is most fully realised in the concluding scenes. We refer not only to those moments when the voice-overs are not immediately or easily attributable, but also to their frequently taking the form of an address to a floating or unidentifiable 'you'. Early in the film, as the men move through the jungle toward their battle position, we hear Witt's voice asking: 'Who are you who lives with all these many forms?' Is he addressing a pantheistic spirit in nature who is the 'source of all that's going to be born'? The attributes of this godlike source of life are 'glory, mercy, peace, truth', and it gives 'calm spirit, understanding, courage, the contented heart'. But is this spirit mortal? – 'your death', Witt enigmatically says, 'that captures all.' Later, Witt stares at the head of a Japanese soldier emerging from the earth in which the rest of his body is buried, and it seems to be the dead man's voice who asks Witt (or who asks us?): 'Are you righteous, kind? … Are you loved by all? Know that I was too. Do you imagine your suffering will be less because you loved goodness, truth?' Much later, it is Bell's voice that takes up the questioning, questioning about the origin of love (inspired, in his case, by love for his wife): 'How do we get to those other shores? Love … where does it come from? … I was a prisoner, you set me free.' The address becomes most

mysterious just a few moments before the film ends. As the soldiers walk past a military cemetery on their way to the ship that will take them from Guadalcanal, we hear what appears to be Top's voice. Following his sombre voice-over commentary during the new Captain's address to the company ('You're in a moving box'; the only thing a man can do is 'find something that's his, make an island for himself'), Top now voices a yearning for something he lacks but to which he would give his life: 'If I never meet you in this life, let me feel the lack. A glance from your eyes and my life will be yours.' Is this 'you' a person, someone who might be loved? This seems unlikely, given the unhappy dénouement of the film's only example of passionate love for another person. The 'you' here becomes more credible as an allegorising of the 'glory' Top had always claimed not to know – as if, at the very depths of a pessimism justified by everything that has happened (the violence, the falsity of official speech, and especially the loss of comrades, of Witt), Top had suddenly come to need and even to believe so strongly in Witt's 'other world' that to feel the pain of *not* living in it, of not seeing its 'glory', had become the most precious thing he can imagine. Finally, as the ship pulls away, and as we see a matured, even

distinguished-looking Doll (Dash Mihok) standing alone at the railing – remarkably changed from the brash, gaping-mouthed, recklessly courageous boy who had, in battle, shouted his pride at having just killed for the first time – Witt's voice returns to speak the film's most perplexing, most resonant lines:

> Where is it that we were together? Who were you that I lived with, walked with? – the brother, the friend. Darkness, light, strife and love, are they the workings of one mind, the features of the same face? Oh my soul, let me be in you now. Look out through my eyes, look out at the things you made. All things shinin'.

Have Witt's friends become unidentifiable *after* their having lived together: is the place where they fought together now unlocatable? Then the notion we have heard before of two worlds, one good and one evil, a world of darkness and a world of light, returns, modified, as the opposed features of the same face. The final 'you' is the speaker's soul – a soul, strangely, that is his but that is external to him, one he prays to enter. And yet his soul is already within him; he even lends it his eyes so that it can look out at its creation. Is the world the creation of a soul living in one man, but to which that man himself may not have had access until now – a single soul that has made a world as we have never seen it but which *is* the visible world, where all things are perpetually shining?

Because *The Thin Red Line* is *cinematically* indifferent to the philosophical questions it schematically asks (what is the origin of evil? how are good and evil related?), we hesitate to impose an arbitrary conceptual clarity on the film's final moments. These voice-overs do, however, appear to be working toward a verbal formulation of the all-inclusive receptiveness of Witt's look. The world can be made by the soul that 'looks' at it. Since the film never puts into question the objective existence of the natural, non-human world, it can be said that the soul has made the world not in the sense of having shaped it into the reflection of a human psyche, but rather simply by virtue of welcoming its appearances. That welcome, which is all that can be read in Witt's look (his look is never a window onto psychic depths), is not the sign of a decision *about* the world; it acknowledges an inescapable connectedness, the fact that I *am* only *in the world*. I move within my repeated, disseminated being.

The inaccurate replications scattered throughout the film propose an ontology of universal immanence: the surfaces of all things 'quiver' from the presence within them of all the other things to which they relate. There is, indeed, as Witt insists, another world, but it is *this* world seen as a vast reservoir of correspondences, of surfaces always ready to 'open' in order to acknowledge, to welcome, to receive that which is at once their outer and their immanent being. This is how we understand 'all things shinin'': all the play with light in *The Thin Red Line* – not only the sun's rays passing through and being dispersed by the high branches of trees, but also the flames of fires raging through villages, as well as the verbal references to love's flame and to the spark that signals a closeness to the 'glory' – represents and refers to all these reflecting surfaces. Surfaces blurred, made somewhat indeterminate by the light shining on them, are visual metaphors for the indeterminate identity conferred on all things by inaccurate replication. The ungraspable nature of reflected being is also emphasised by the importance of water in the film: all the images of swirling water, the soldiers' need for water (a need dismissed by the Colonel), the happiness of the men bathing after the battle and of Witt swimming underwater with his Melanesian friends. Light and water become figures for the universal circularity of being, a circularity also repeated by the philosophical reflections in the film, reflections that go nowhere, make no argument but, instead, address the issues they raise by their very insistence, by the different moments of reflective thought reflecting (repeating and revising) other moments.

The perplexing allusion to a soul that the speaking subject seeks to enter but that is also invited to look at the world it has made through that same subject's eyes – as if the 'I' could be both internal and external to its own soul, and as if this spirit that is his were indistinguishable from that which is external to them both – all this becomes intelligible in terms of an ontology that treats as merely incidental, as a by-product of the illusion of individuality, the opposition between the outside and the inside. The 'you' of the voice-overs is, finally, more of a trap than an enigma. It leads us to want to pinpoint 'who' it is, whereas the connectedness we have been speaking of – Witt's visual absorption of all that is – dissolves the separate identity that a 'who' falsely presupposes. There can be no answers to the questions: 'Where is it that we were together? Who were you that I lived with?' Like 'you', these questions create a false distance, and their superfluity is suggested by the fact that all the speech in *The Thin Red Line* that seeks individualising identifications (who put evil in the world? who were you that I lived with?) gets nowhere, can be uttered only as incantatory interrogations. These questions are asked not in order to be answered, but in order to help us to understand the extensibility of being that can be voiced only as that which it is not, as that which always fails to be adequate to the film's vision. Love sequesters the objects it at once idealises and impoverishes. The being-togetherness *seen* by *The Thin Red Line* – a condition that makes no essential distinction between the human and the non-human – assumes the capacity of all objects to be less than what each one is, and therefore to participate (as witnessed by an active seeing) in the community of all being.

★ ★ ★

Finally, however, as an implicated witness of the world, Witt is also, inevitably, a melancholy witness. The connectedness that is the source of his joy also makes it impossible for him to be detached from the governing illusion of the world: the illusion of *dis*connectedness. That illusion, embraced by Freud, makes of the external world, according to the founder of psycho-analysis, an always potentially dangerous enemy of the self. 'At the very beginning,' Freud writes in the 1915 essay 'Instincts and Their Vicissitudes', 'the external world, objects, and what is hated are identical.' Not only at the very beginning: 'As an expression of the reaction of unpleasure evoked by objects,' Freud continues, 'hate always remains in an intimate relation with the self-preservative instincts.'[11] *Civilisation and Its Discontents* elaborates these statements in the form of a sustained and powerful argument against Romain Rolland's interpretation of an 'oceanic feeling' of ecstatic oneness with the world. In the first chapter of that work, Freud dismisses the oceanic feeling as a delusionary cure for human suffering traceable to the 'limitless narcissism' of infancy.[12] Instead of oneness, there is, Freud argues, an intractable hostility between the human subject and the world, although, curiously, 'the blindest fury of destructiveness' is accompanied by an ecstatic sense of having broken down the barriers between the self and the world. This psychoanalytic ecstasy is not, however, Rolland's joyful religious union with the universe, but rather accompanies the illusion of an omnipotent aggressiveness that would destroy the world as such, the world as distinct from (and distinctly hostile to) the human ego.

The pervasive melancholy of *The Thin Red Line* is the affective sign of what Malick can't help but see as an unavoidable connection to, even participation in, this blind fury of destructiveness. Motivated by a conviction of the profoundly hostile *difference* of the world, the subject wars against that difference, and the world that harbours it. The melancholic inflection of Witt's witnessing is the sign of his having to include that which would kill in order definitively to exclude. Malick's film, we might even say, stacks the cards against Witt's sense of 'glory', of 'all things shinin''. He cruelly tests that sense by immersing it in the experience of war, of unceasing murder, thereby forcing Witt, as it were, to invent 'another world' in which what he claims to see might find a place to be. Malick's camera lingers on the lovely images of nature at peace only, it sometimes seems, in order to destroy the quiet with the suddenly all-intrusive noises of battle. Also, some of the grimmest scenes are made even grimmer by being silenced. We don't hear the voices of the visibly screaming, emaciated, defeated Japanese soldiers as the camera circles among them; rather, the image is accompanied by Witt's voice, against a background of extended, low musical chords, asking how this evil got into the world. The horror of the image is heightened by the absence of any sound emerging from it. The devastated bodies are merely exposed, without even being allowed to give voice to their humiliated humanity. These are not the only *unspeakable* images in *The Thin Red Line*. There is Bell, so shattered by the chaos and the violence of the fighting that has just ended, as well as by his own terror, that when Doll approaches him he moves his lips to address him but is unable to utter a sound; the two soldiers' wordless embrace is not a celebration of victory, but looks more like the tender acknowledgment of a shared brokenness. Perhaps the most haunting image of all is that of the soldier who had taunted one of the dying Japanese prisoners, and whom we later see sitting under the rain, half naked, shaking uncontrollably, wholly alone, visibly sobbing but cut off from the film's sound-track, severed even from the comfort of the rosary he seems furiously to fling away from himself.

Defeated dogs, Witt might say (he speaks of war turning men into dogs), and they have to be included in his absorption of all that is, in his letting the world be. For that 'allowance' has to include all that would exclude any allowance. The fact that the reoccurrences – the inaccurate replications that design the mobile oneness of the world, and *our* oneness with the world – naturally include threats to this being-togetherness is casually figured in the film's final visual similitude. The verticality of the rifle a soldier on the departing ship is holding, and which he looks down at, is repeated in the film's final image, that of two coconut shoots rising from the shallow water. It is an affectively and morally neutral image, even more so than that of the crocodile in the opening scene, an image made portentous by the long low musical chord that accompanies the animal's descent into

the water. But portentous of what? The crocodile of course searches for prey, but it is not presented as a menace, and later we see soldiers surrounding a captured crocodile, touching it, it would seem, with a certain curiosity. These are interestingly insignificant images; perhaps the crocodile doesn't 'signify' any more than the coconut shoots, except as a presence, one that other presences can take note of, perhaps touch, to which they might have a certain physical or formal connectedness.

Perhaps *The Thin Red Line* suggests that the 'resolution' to the problem of evil, in this instance the evil of war, lies in nothing more dramatic than the recognition of this connectedness. Some would undoubtedly say: nothing more effective. It is true that this resolution, in Malick's film, takes the form of, can go no further than, an aesthetic demonstration – a truth tacitly acknowledged by the film's pervasive melancholy. Can total acceptance be distinguished from total passivity? The question is tendentious, since it implicitly accuses passivity of failing to respond to the evil it registers. This passivity would thus be a moral (and, it goes without saying, a political) failure. But, as we have meant to suggest in our discussion of *The Thin Red Line*, the perceptual aesthetic of film can be ethically defended. It registers not the real world 'as it is', but a positioning *in* a real world. The images of film propose relational models, which means that film can't help but work within the field of ethics. To play against the sense of a playful remark by Godard in *Le Vent d'est* (1969 – repeated in *Histoire(s) du cinéma*): to say that the cinematic image is just an image may lead us to ask to what extent it is a just image. Psychoanalysis describes the human drive to destroy relations; *jouissance* 'rewards' the illusion of having abolished the distance, and the difference, between the subject and the world. Witt's absorptions have nothing to do with this murderous ecstasy. On the contrary: they enhance the world's existence – give it its shining aspect – by never ceasing to locate him within it. To be that extraordinarily receptive to the being of the world is perhaps inevitably to be shattered by it (an onto-

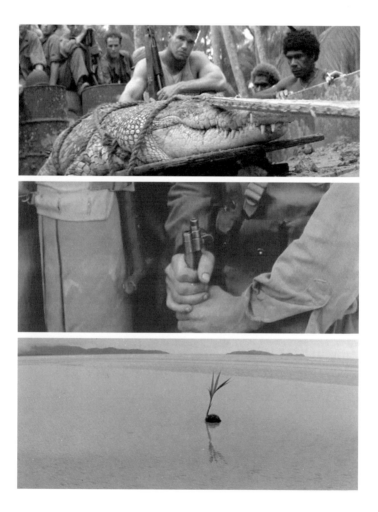

logical truth that Witt's death metaphorises) – shattered in order to be recycled as allness. Inaccurate replications – between the subject and the world, among the world's objects – shatter individual identities in order to redesign the world as correspondences that can be illuminated by our perception of them. To open ourselves to those correspondences requires a relational discipline capable of yielding an ascetic pleasure that may, at least intermittently, supersede the *jouissance* of 'the blindest fury of destructiveness'. War, and the *jouissance* that nourishes war, contradicts universal presence. To *show* this is art's highest ethical accomplishment. Allness, as the wholly open looking of Malick's magnificent film[13] teaches us, is the truest human ripeness.

Notes

1. Sigmund Freud, *Civilisation and Its Discontents*, trans. James Strachey (New York: W. W. Norton, 1961), pp. 69–70.

2. Jacques Lacan, *The Ethics of Psychoanalysis*, in Jacques-Alain Miller (ed.), *The Seminar of Jacques Lacan 1959–60*, trans. Dennis Porter (London: Routledge, 1992), p. 179.

3. Freud, *Civilisation and Its Discontents*, p. 81.

4. Lacan, *The Ethics of Psychoanalysis*, pp. 187, 186 and 184.

5. Freud, *Civilisation and Its Discontents*, p. 81.

6. Nothing could be more different from the vastly more popular and wholly mediocre *Saving Private Ryan*, Steven Spielberg's 1998 flag-waving epic.

7. In a brilliant juxtaposition of Malick's film with Heidegger's reflections on 'Being-toward-death ... more a way of inhabiting the world than of leaving it', Kaja Silverman emphasises 'Witt's decision

to live "toward" his finitude through his early meditation upon his own death.' See Silverman, 'All Things Shining', in David L. Eng and David Kazanjian (eds), *Loss/The Politics of Mourning* (Berkeley: University of California Press, 2003), pp. 326, 336.

8. Most of the shots we will be discussing are not, technically speaking, exactly close-ups, but are rather medium close-ups. It is, however, the face that entirely absorbs our attention.

9. Oppositional but also juxtaposed: the terms of each couple co-exist within this world.

10. The relation between the individual members of a group and the group's leader is famously theorised by Freud in *Group Psychology and the Analysis of the Ego* (1921).

11. Freud, 'Instincts and Their Vicissitudes' (1915), in *The Standard Edition of the Complete Psychological Works of Sigmund Freud*, trans. and ed. James Strachey, 24 vols (London: Hogarth, 1953–74), vol. 14, pp. 136, 139.

12. Freud, *Civilisation and Its Discontents*, p. 20.

13. A film immeasurably superior to the rather ordinary war novel that 'inspired' it: James Jones's 1962 novel of the same title. In particular, neither Top nor Witt has anything approaching the interest and originality of those figures in Malick's film.

Picture Credits

Le Mépris / Il disprezzo / Contempt (chapter 1 and plate section): directed by Jean-Luc Godard, © Rome–Paris Films, Paris / Films Concordia (Paris) / Campagnia Cinematografica Champion, 1963. DVD available from Momentum Pictures Home Entertainment (UK, 2004), The Criterion Collection under exclusive license from StudioCanal Image (USA, 2002).

Michelangelo Merisi da Caravaggio (1571–1610), *Bacchino Malato*, *c.* 1593, Rome, Galleria Borghese (p. 38, top). *Boy with a Basket of Fruit*, 1593–4, Rome, Galleria Borghese (p. 38, bottom).

Mon oncle d'Amérique / My American Uncle (pp. 44–5): directed by Alain Resnais, © Andrea Films / T.F.1 Films Productions (Paris), 1980. DVD available from mk2 (France, 2003).

Todo sobre mi madre / All About My Mother (chapter 2 and plate section): directed by Pedro Almodóvar, © El Deseo / Renn Productions / France 2 Cinéma, 1999. DVD available from Pathé Distribution (UK, 2000), Columbia Tristar (US, 2000).

The Thin Red Line (chapter 3 and plate section): directed by Terrence Malick, © Twentieth Century Fox Film Corporation, 1998. DVD available from Twentieth Century Fox Home Entertainment (UK, 2000 / US, 1999).

Index